An Interpretive Introduction *to* Western Religions

An Interpretive Introduction to Western Religions

Amir Sabzevary

WIPF & STOCK · Eugene, Oregon

AN INTERPRETIVE INTRODUCTION TO WESTERN RELIGIONS

Copyright © 2022 Amir Sabzevary. All rights reserved. Except for brief quotations in critical publications or reviews, no part of this book may be reproduced in any manner without prior written permission from the publisher. Write: Permissions, Wipf and Stock Publishers, 199 W. 8th Ave., Suite 3, Eugene, OR 97401.

Wipf & Stock
An Imprint of Wipf and Stock Publishers
199 W. 8th Ave., Suite 3
Eugene, OR 97401

www.wipfandstock.com

PAPERBACK ISBN: 978-1-6667-3770-7
HARDCOVER ISBN: 978-1-6667-9744-2
EBOOK ISBN: 978-1-6667-9745-9

APRIL 19, 2022 1:14 PM

Scripture quotations are from the Revised Standard Version of the Bible, copyright © 1946, 1952, and 1971 National Council of the Churches of Christ in the United States of America. Used by permission. All rights reserved worldwide.

Contents

INTRODUCTION TO RELIGIOUS TRADITIONS | 1
    Gilgamesh | 2
    Hinduism | 5
    Buddhism | 8
    Taoism | 10
    Confucianism | 12

1 JUDAISM | 15
    The Story of Moses | 15
    The Garden of Eden | 21
    The Ten Commandments | 25
    The Book of Job | 36

2 CHRISTIANITY | 47
    The Gospel of Mark | 48
    The Gospel of Matthew | 54
    The Gospel of Luke | 58
    The Gospel of John | 61
    The Gospel of Judas | 62
    Christian Philosophy | 63
    Christianity and Modern Society | 71
    Forgiveness | 74

3   Islam | 82

    The Life of Mohammed | 82

    What Does It Mean to Be Human in Islam? | 86

    The Five Pillars of Islam | 91

    How Do You Fast from Experiences? | 101

    Why Should We Fast from Experiences?
    Why Can't We Turn Them into Tools for Wisdom? | 103

    How Do You Protect Yourself from Social Forces,
    and What Is Praying for Yourself? | 103

    How Did Religious Culture Become Secular, and Is It Possible
    for Society to Become Once Again More Religious? | 105

    Poverty in Islam | 111

Bibliography | 115

Introduction to Religious Traditions

ONE DAY A MAN decides to go to India to visit some friends. The Middle Eastern or Near Eastern cultures demand that they always bring something back for friends, relatives, and those close to them whenever someone goes on vacation.

The Persian poet Rumi tells a story about a man wanting to go to India.[1] Having only a minute before leaving for his trip, he suddenly remembers his parrot, a beautiful bird that lives in a cage. He asks the bird if there is anything she wants from India. The bird tells her owner that she would like him to go to a place called Dehradun, where he will see a gigantic tree on whose branches sit similar-looking birds that sing and fly around the tree. He should tell those birds that he has a bird that lives in a cage but cannot fly because the cage is too small and cannot sing because there is no one to listen to her. So, the bird sits, alone and sad.

Although the owner thinks this is a strange request, he nevertheless honors it. So before returning home from India, he goes to the designated place to fulfill his bird's request. Upon seeing him, the birds tell the man that he is standing on sacred grounds and should immediately leave. Before leaving, the man tells them that he has a bird that looks like them at home. She wants to fly but cannot because the cage is too small and wants to sing but doesn't because there is hardly anyone there to listen to her.

One bird sitting high in the tree falls to the ground and dies upon hearing the tale. Shocked and saddened, the man leaves and returns home. When he enters his home, the bird asks him if he visited Dehradun and talked to the birds. After telling his bird what happened in India, the bird falls to the bottom of the cage and dies. Saddened that he has killed two birds, the man opens the cage and gently grabs the bird to go to the garden

---

1. Nicholson, *Mathnawi of Jalaluddin Rumi*.

to bury her. He puts the bird on the ground and starts digging a hole. To his surprise, the moment the bird is placed on the floor, she flies away.

The story seems simple, but it is filled with profound subtleties about the human condition that many religious traditions express differently. The human flesh and the politics of life silence the bird, or the spirit that lives within the human being, and clips its wings so that it can remain in exile, unhappy and dissatisfied.

Consider those moments we fall in love: this cage called the human body and human expectations gets in the way and ruins the magic and the baptism of love. Sometimes we want to write essays. We are inspired because our wings are flapping and our spirits are singing, but our instructors demand something different. Slowly, fear overshadows inspiration. Our flesh's desire for grade, money, or social status overtakes the desires of our souls. Inspiration goes away. We are silenced, and our wings stop flapping.

Let me translate and share another poem by the same poet, Rumi. "Upon waking up, I ask: Why am I here? What sort of an animal am I? What is my purpose? Why is it that every time I remember to live a purposive, meaningful life, I fall into forgetfulness?"[2] All these spiritual questions that are the focus of the major religious traditions fall victim to this cage called the human body, the senses, the desires, and the politics of society. Ultimately the bird is silenced, and all that remains of human beings are unexamined social obligations.

Before we talk about Judaism, Christianity, and Islam, and how each would respond to restoring the human spirit, it would be helpful to briefly review some Eastern religious traditions such as the Epic of Gilgamesh, Hinduism, Buddhism, Taoism, and Confucianism.

Gilgamesh

In the Epic of Gilgamesh, we are told that Gilgamesh becomes forgetful of his soul's purpose because he's so physically attractive and powerful.[3] And also because he's a king. But because the gods favor him and want him to remember who he is so that he can experience the divinity within him, they make plans to break him. The suggestion is that the gods tell us something every time we are broken. Because we too are favored by them.

---

2. Nicholson, *Mathnawi of Jalaluddin Rumi*.
3. Sandars and Pasco, *Epic of Gilgamesh*.

Introduction to Religious Traditions

When our hearts are broken, the only thing that matters to us is finding ways to mend our hearts and put the pieces back together. Everything else in life becomes irrelevant. When something in us is severely broken, it forces us to kneel; it forces our ego to disappear to have the right set of emotions and thoughts, enabling us to ask the right questions.

There is something that has always lived inside Gilgamesh that says, to paraphrase, "I don't want to die, and I don't want to be forgotten. I want to be immortal. I don't want to be a book that stays on a shelf and gathers dust. I want to be opened, and I want to be read because my story is exciting and inspiring. It speaks of the human soul." That is what Gilgamesh wants. However, since he is drunk with physical power and because all of his desires are rooted in physical power, everything about him is expressed in all the wrong ways. He harasses and abuses people; he violates and dishonors women. After the gods receive many complaints from his people, they intervene. The gods realize that there is only one way for Gilgamesh, the archetypal human being, to be inspired. There is only one way for a human being to experience a meaningful and lasting transformation. The gods do not want inspirations that only last a minute and then disappear into oblivion.

The gods allow Gilgamesh to fall in love with a person named Enkidu. It is only through this particular kind of love that his soul, which was hidden, invisible, or forgotten, reveals itself and becomes visible. Gilgamesh ultimately becomes charitable and generous to his people through this kind of love. Love toward the rights creates a particular type of attachment that births trust and faith, leading to complete and lasting inner transformation. Trust and faith, however, are not created or willed by Gilgamesh. Instead, they happened to him through the gods' desire and will.

When you say to someone, "I have fallen in love," the truth is you have done nothing on your own because you don't fall in love through your effort. Consider love as a gift or a grace from the heavens or gods. Something falls into your life, something about you opens up, you receive this other person, and this other person, again without your will, subtly makes you generous, compassionate, and forgiving. Next time you wait for a text to come your way, *you* are not waiting, but love allows and enables you to wait. Through love, you have acquired one of the names of God in the Islamic tradition, Patience.[4]

---

4. Helminski and Rezwani, *Love's Ripening*.

It is important to note that Gilgamesh's transformation is through co-dependency founded in love. Enkidu means "the most innocent of mankind."[5] Something profoundly sacred that lives in us can only come to life in the presence of someone who's profoundly innocent. It is only in the presence of this otherworldly innocence that we can be reminded of the divinity within. Gilgamesh falls in love and becomes immensely attached to Enkidu, but, unbeknownst to him, the gods had already decided that Enkidu must die, which would initiate Gilgamesh toward the spiritual quest. Unlike the rest of us, who enjoy distracting ourselves from devastating existential questions that the presence and the awareness of death bring about, Gilgamesh is willing to live with those questions and the pain they generate.

Embracing Enkidu while he takes his last breath pushes Gilgamesh to the world of reflection and introspection. He wants something that cannot be destroyed by the cruel hands of time. He wants to fall in love with something eternal and immortal. He comes to realize that there is only one way to have this lasting romance that is out of life's reach: self-romance. That is self-governed by the immortal nature of wisdom, out of which love and compassion arise.

Gilgamesh goes on a long journey. An arduous exodus. A long desert life. He goes through many difficult tests. He has to prove himself to the scorpion men who stand guard outside the gates of the sun god Shamash at the mountains of Mashu, to the wise cosmic barmaid Siduri, and finally to the mysterious boatsmen Urshanabi, who takes him across the Waters of Death to the Far-Away Place. He must pass all these tests to become a worthy seeker after truth. Once in the presence of King Utnapishtim, which means, "He who has found life," Gilgamesh is told that the search for truth is a solitary journey and no one can give wisdom to another. According to the king, wisdom doesn't come from mortals but rather from the gods. Gilgamesh is told of a plant of immortality that grows at the bottom of a river. He must find the river, swim to the bottom, find the plant and eat it. Once he consumes it, he will become immortal.

Gilgamesh, for the most part, does as he is told. He has a change of heart. He does not eat the plant. Instead, he wants to go back to his people and educate them about love, life, and death. It is about living a life that is worth living and remembering. As the Hindus would say, he realizes that

---

5. Sandars and Pasco, *Epic of Gilgamesh*.

people, as they ordinarily are, live in *Maya*, or the world of illusions.[6] They pursue and desire the wrong things in hopes of finding this thing called "happiness." Gilgamesh realizes that as long as illusions are sought, sadness and regret soon follow. Gilgamesh sacrifices his immortality for his people. This is no different from Malcolm X's life, no different from the life of Mahatma Gandhi, no different from the life of Jesus Christ. They all went through the same episodes. They all had their quest, which was filled with fear, doubt, and loneliness. Despite their anguish, these heroes discovered a truth that made them a prophet for their people.

The Gilgamesh story speaks of something profoundly sacred that lived inside us, which could only manifest itself through love, loss, grief, and reflection.

It is this caged sacred bird that religious traditions argue lives inside all of us, but which gets covered under an avalanche of nonsensical instinctual as well as manufactured desires and ambitions. In the Epic of Gilgamesh, a baptism rooted in love and loss is necessary to liberate this bird or our soul. A baptism throws us into a desert experience, an initiation into the spiritual life. But there are no guarantees that we will reach our goal! The human being either dies in the desert or finds an oasis.

Hinduism

In Hinduism, it is argued that the spiritual quest involves our search for *atman*, the "real self." This thing in us is immortal and refuses to be contaminated by the world. It is, if you will, the "kingdom of God within us." However, self-love is necessary for *atman* to be realized, which is not as easy as we may think. Hinduism argues that we become like an onion over our life, wearing layer upon layer of masks or false personalities to survive in the politics of life. Such masks as being a student, a father, a mother, a waiter, or a waitress. After a while, we think that we are these layers or masks. Each mask creates its own set of unique questions, interests, desires, ambitions, insecurities, fears, and doubts. Even if we find all the answers to the questions raised by one layer, there are many more layers to tackle. Since one lifetime is simply not enough to tackle all the questions, Hinduism asks us to eliminate all these questions and layers and *get to the essence*. Those are questions, desires, and ambitions that live in our souls. Forget, for example, what it means to be gay or straight, black or white, as all these

6. Smith, *World's Religions*.

are distracting questions; instead, ask, "What does it mean to be a human being?" It embodies all the questions that relate to human beings.

Hinduism argues that it's nearly impossible to wrestle with questions in the right way during the first forty years of life because we are trying to fulfill social demands and responsibilities. As children, we are consumed by curiosity, so we walk around trying to open all the boxes we see in the world to see what's inside them. Then we enter the academic world, where we have to prove how smart we are. Life revolves around money, power, social status, marriage, and children.

By the age of fifty, we have tasted the pleasures that money, power, marriage, and parenthood bring about. Once we have experienced some of the joys that the physical world has to offer, suddenly something strange happens to us. We sit back and ask, "That's it? Really? All that work, and for what?" These questions, according to Hinduism, push us into our desert life, which they call the "renunciation" or "retirement" stage. A stage where we go into a room trying to figure out what went wrong in our life. To try to understand why so much time and energy were wasted in the pursuit of trivial things.

Atman is the bird hidden under an avalanche of masks or false personalities but now wants to free itself. She wants to fly and sing freely. But first she needs to find a way to free herself from the bondage of all these other layers, the false personalities. The Hindus argue that once we get to a place of discontent, sadness, anger, and depression, like Gilgamesh, we hear a voice that says, to paraphrase, "Seek Utnapishtim, the man who found life and who is the source of wisdom." In Hinduism, the voice that you hear says, "Seek a guru, someone who can rid you of your illusions about yourself and life, someone who can get rid of your childish fantasies and false hopes." Once you find a teacher, the seeker falls into different stages.

First, the seeker, you, feels a strange sense of intimacy with this teacher for some peculiar reason. This person you just met. All you know is that it seems like your soul is connected to this person in some strange way. This person becomes your home. However, it is an environment where conflicting feelings, desires, emotions, and thoughts exist. This person becomes your worst enemy and your best friend. Teachers, generally, introduce you to a different aspect of yourself—a more refined, mature, and self-aware aspect. At the same time, this new self also witnesses the old self. The one you have lived with for many years and with which you have decades of history. It is not easy to get rid of that history, all the attachments to historical emotions, thoughts, and habits.

We are ready to work with a teacher who can transform us from within. The first thing that will happen is that we fall in love with the teacher. They call it *bhakti-yoga*. You merge with the teacher and become one with them. It is a sort of love with vital components of fear and doubt, joy and sorrow. Despite the conflicting feelings, if the love is strong enough, the relationship between the teacher and student grows.

Once a person falls in love with the teacher, they enter the second stage. Here they are forced into psychological seclusion, eventually bringing about physical isolation. During this stage, sadness grows, communicating with others falls apart, and joy and comfort leave. The individual becomes incredibly alone and depressed. This pain, however, brings about single-mindedness and focus. Nothing can be done in this stage except to be around the teacher, the guru, who has the power to remove these layers of an onion or false personalities slowly. The teacher gradually guides the student towards self-sufficiency, where ultimately the student becomes a guide to him- or herself. This is called *raja yoga*.

Next, the guru shares with the student this thing called *jnana yoga*, or "nuggets of wisdom." However, it is essential to note that the teacher only gives and can only give the sort of wisdom indispensable to the student's emotional, intellectual, and spiritual needs and growth. But for that to happen, this person—your teacher, for example—needs to get to know you extremely well. The teacher may say things or do things that may seem intrusive, unethical, and immoral to the student. However, if the teacher is authentic, sincere, and has wisdom, the student's perception of the teacher is transformed over time. Actions that the student deemed or categorized as wrong or negative become the source of understanding and transformation.

While being trained by the teacher, the student is forced to observe *dharma yoga*, or ethical codes designed to bring about understanding, wisdom, and autonomy. Whatever the teacher does and asks for is for the sake of student's emotional, intellectual, and spiritual growth. Eventually, after the teacher, *dharma yoga* leads the student to serve people in whatever shape and form possible. At this stage, the student no longer pursues God or wisdom. There is no longer a need for solitude and seclusion. There are no books to read and no people to listen to. The student has entered a stage of *pantheism*. Everything has a spark of divinity, and therefore everything has something to offer and teach. At this stage, the student's awareness enables them to learn from life.

There is a story from the book *Hermit* about a man of wisdom who lived on top of Mount Athos. His visitors are only those who want to resolve their physical issues. Now, you may think that teachers of wisdom only share their wisdom to lead people toward God, enlightenment, understanding the meaning and purpose of their own life, and liberating their soul from the bondage of the material world. That you want to teach people, as Jesus states in the Gospel of Mark 8:36, "What benefit is there for someone to gain the whole world and lose his soul?" Teachers, however, soon realize that people are not yet that advanced, and they want to resolve the everyday issues of life that birth emotional and mental anguish.

Buddhism

The story in the Buddhist tradition begins with a man named Siddhartha, who, very much like us, desires and wants the kingdom of the physical world so that he can experience and taste all the pleasures therein.[7] The story is about all of us who want to be a CEO or the next Steve Jobs. Like the rest of us, he imagines himself as unique, talented, and invincible.

However, loneliness sets in slowly, and, like the rest of us, he gets married. Then loneliness sets in within the marriage. Like the rest of us, he has children. Then at a certain point, every person, very much like Siddhartha, the to-be Buddha, looks at their life and says, "I have given my energy to my wife or my husband, I've given my energy to my children, and I've given my energy to various social branches; what happened to me? In giving myself away to these things, I have forgotten one significant person, and that's myself. I will get old, and I will get sick. I will die and then be forgotten." Very much like Gilgamesh, Siddhartha wants to be remembered, but not as a good husband or wife, or as a good father or a good CEO. He wants to be remembered as someone immortal, someone eternal, someone who reached this thing called "wisdom." And as someone whose life was meaningful enough that it was worth remembering and talking about.

He realizes that if wisdom cannot be obtained through physical life, perhaps he should try becoming spiritual. So he becomes religious, which meant following the path of Hinduism in his time. However, he realizes that although it is nice to hold your breath for ten minutes, to levitate, in

---

7. Smith, *World's Religions*.

the end, these are passing experiences, and all that remains is a memory. He doesn't want to sit somewhere and have memories of these incredible experiences. He says, "Life is a living organism, and I want to be part of it. I don't want to sit on the bleachers and watch life go by; I want to participate in it in a meaningful way, but I do not even know what that means. Physical life hasn't helped. Religious and spiritual life haven't helped. What do I do?"

His perception of physical as well as spiritual life becomes dark and gloomy. He observes life and concludes that it is no good. But why?

Consider the following. Everything new gradually becomes old and then starts to sicken you, ending in indifference toward it. And you sit and ask, "Did I have to spend all this time pursuing things which in the end hold no meaning for me?" So, in the end, Siddhartha, not yet the Buddha, sits in isolation and despair. There is no one to talk to and nothing to do. "I cannot find nourishment in religion or physical life."[8] He is simply a broken man.

There is a saying in Islam that "If you want God to come down, you must have a heart that is broken." And, that is precisely what happens to Siddhartha. And his message for the rest of us is, to paraphrase, "Enjoy life, since there is nothing wrong with it. But know that a coffin sits next to the birth of every new thing, and you will have to bury every experience. They will live in memory and are retrieved upon remembrance. Be happy but know that the sibling of happiness is sorrow." You should be happy that you're going to get married, but also be sad because the newness and the excitement of the marriage will leave you and most of what is left is the politics of surviving the relationship. Be happy that you will have children, but the newness will leave. Soon you will realize that, despite your best efforts, society will eventually take them and shape them.

Once he becomes the Buddha, or a wise teacher of the physical and the spiritual realms, he gives us four important lessons. In the Buddhist tradition, they are called the Four Nobles Truths. The first is that everything in life will eventually die and leave us mourning. We feel betrayed, and we are left in sadness and sorrow. We will suffer. This is because, ultimately, impermanence reigns supreme over all things. The second is that suffering is caused by desire. In pursuing the object of desire, we form a physical, emotional, and intellectual relationship that creates strong attachments. Attachments create emotional and mental memories. You may have a failed marriage, and although your ex is no longer around, you think and feel

---

8. Aflaki, *Rumi and His Friends*.

about them, either negatively or positively. The truth is that the mental image of the marriage will haunt you. Or your ex-companion's abuse will haunt you. Or that you can't find anyone as good as them will haunt you. These emotional memories arise because of attachment. The third and the fourth truths are the remedies to the first two. The third is to know that there is a way where suffering and attachment can end. It ends by following and being aware of eight steps.

The first step is about *understanding*. That is, making sure that you know life embodies impermanence. Once you understand this truth, you reach the second step, *thoughtfulness*. You begin to *think* about your physical, emotional, intellectual, and spiritual relationships properly. That is, without wrong expectations that could lead to attachments. Your understanding and thoughtfulness lead to the third step, *speech*. Make sure that whatever you say expresses thoughtfulness within the context of understanding the nature of life, which is impermanence. Also, know that speech cannot manipulate others for self-gain. Just in case you have nothing to say, according to the Buddha, it is best to observe "noble silence," or keep one's mouth shut. The fourth step is making sure that all of your *actions* are in the service of your emotional, intellectual, and spiritual growth. Your actions must always contain the proper understanding and thoughtfulness. Do not allow yourself to act in any way that would birth regret and shame.

The fifth step is *livelihood*. The ways we try to make rent, provide food, and take care of our parents. Life is expensive. However, satisfying our needs must never come at the expense of hurting or exploiting others. Hence making money by selling drugs or alcohol would not be appropriate. Since human beings are bound to forget these five steps, the sixth step, *effort*, is an alarm clock to remember the first five steps. The sixth step embodies the seventh and the eighth steps, *mindfulness* and *concentration*. That is, paying attention, being aware and focused on everything taking place inside and outside of you—making sure that all eight steps are being appropriately observed.

Since, according to this tradition, the Buddha seed exists in everyone, our task, as human beings, is to make sure that this grows appropriately and thoroughly. These eight steps are there to ensure that.

Introduction to Religious Traditions

Taoism

Then there is Taoism. This tradition argues that there is always a particular flow in life.[9] It is natural and organic. Say you wake up in a certain mood, and your mood happens to be a sad one. But not a sadness that is the outcome of an unprocessed experience, but one that is reflective and introspective. You look yourself in the mirror, and you say, "What am I? Who am I? What happened to my life?" Instead of falling victim to the youth culture of America that encourages running away from these existential questions with cheap and shallow distractions, Taoism asks that you embrace this mood because that is the flow that lives inside you. Sit, read, weep, scream—it doesn't matter how you want to express it, as long as you do justice to the thing that lives inside you. Every human being, Lao Tzu argues, is like a river. This river has a specific flow, and don't ever swim against this flow. If you're born a pianist, don't be a plumber. If you're born a plumber, don't be a pianist. But because none of us have the courage or the awareness about the flow of life; we try to act intelligent but are proven counterfeit, not only by other people but by ourselves. We try to act beautiful, but in the end we become ugly.

How do we baptize the ignorance and arrogance that live inside us, which envelops our lives? Their answer is first to find *water* and then become like water. Water, of course, symbolizes wisdom. One of the qualities of water is that it never seeks high positions as it always flows towards the lowest areas. That is a quality of humility. Also, water always takes the shape of its container—a quality of selflessness. Water never confronts an obstacle directly. Instead, it finds a way to go around it—a quality of intelligent passivity. Remember, you cannot suddenly possess water qualities. Someone who has these qualities must teach and train you. The water needs a container. But the container needs to be *empty*, which is the second quality. Before water or wisdom can be given to anyone, emptiness is required. That is, empty of the self, a collection of historical, cultural, traditional narratives. In addition, there are also personal, physical, emotional, and intellectual narratives and all the desires contained therein. Therefore, a teacher must remove all these narratives, which amount to useless chatter inside the person. Once these narratives or experiences are removed, then emptiness is obtained. One who is empty and possesses wisdom naturally comes to have the third, fourth, and fifth qualities: *innocence, spontaneity,* and *creativity.*

---

9. Smith, *World's Religions.*

Once these five qualities are obtained, one becomes "the way of life," or *tao te*, and will "act without acting," or *wu wei*.

Confucianism

The fifth Far Eastern tradition is called Confucianism, which is very different from the other religious traditions we have talked about so far. Confucius argues that religion and philosophy should provide teachings that help people live a relatively good and comfortable physical life.[10] Marriage, raising children, making money, having friendships, making sure they are healthy, and figuring out who we are and what we should do with our lives are challenging and complicated things. If we define these complexities inappropriately, we will interpret these experiences as unfavorable. Human beings should not live solitary lives. Confucius is the greatest opponent of those cultures and traditions that lead people towards loneliness and despair. For example, when parents get old, make sure that you have a set of traditions that tells children to protect their parents so that they won't find themselves victimized by society and uncaring social systems.

To get rid of loneliness and all the things that create chaos in people's lives, freedom of choice needs to be gotten rid of. Don't give people freedom of choice or options without adequately training them in thinking and feeling about things in the right way. Without proper instructions, people will almost always choose what will eventually harm them and mess up their lives. The remedy is tradition.

Tradition is a set of stories that have been created over the past five thousand years. These stories are not designed or tested by individuals but by time and society. If you give people too many options, they will get confused, and in confusion people suffer from frustration, anxiety, dread, depression, anger, and violence. Keep cities and towns small. Don't let people move to big cities, where they will fall into a state of estrangement, strangeness, invisibility, and insignificance. Instead, let them live in small cities and towns, where everyone knows everyone. In this way, people's relationships are stronger and more intimate. Thus, they will have a vast support system in times of personal crisis. Also, there will be no crime because people will desire to protect their name and reputation. People are not made for big cities, where they get lost, not only in the glimmers of big cities but also in the desires and ambitiousness that big cities create.

10. Confucius, *Analects*.

Introduction to Religious Traditions

Big cities blitz people with an insane number of advertisements, always luring them towards something. If people want to have a relatively healthy life, they must have the right desires. Most important are marriage and children. Marriage will protect you against loneliness, depression, and isolation. It is also beneficial for your mental health.

Make sure, however, that you marry a person because they come from a relatively healthy background, such as having good parents and having a healthy relationship with their parents. Do not marry for love. Love is an intense emotion that blinds you. In blindness, regret, shame, guilt, and anger will eventually follow when important life-changing decisions are made. Also, let marriage be about creating good and healthy children to become healthy and beneficial members of society. Parents also need to sacrifice their desires for the well-being of their marriage and their children. Once you are married, you stay married, in sickness and health. Once you have children, you remain married for their sake. And should you find someone else more attractive, you will kill your passion for that person. You don't want to infect your village and society with constantly changing emotions, such as love. You certainly don't want to create emotional traumas for your kids.

Remember, life is about an extraordinary kind of happiness: stability. Mainly because life is naturally always moving and changing, and marriage, family, respect, and honor are the only things that bring about stability. Always keep in mind the five most important relationships that will protect your life. First, men and women have their unique *roles* in society and marriage. Those roles are defined by tradition. Men support the family by making money, and women support society by ensuring their children are raised properly. Then, there is the *respect* that children must always have for their parents. They must follow their parents' guidance to avoid unnecessary life difficulties. As parents sacrifice their desire for the sake of their children, children must also be trained to sacrifice their childish desires as to not tarnish their family's name. The third kind of relationship that must be honored is the *honor* and *respect* that siblings must have and show towards each other. Remember, this is especially true for younger siblings' interaction with the older ones. It must be noted that, unlike the Western American attitude that "age is just a number," age is equivalent to experience, knowledge, and wisdom in the Chinese tradition. Having learned the proper way to behave towards one's parents and siblings, the individual enters the fourth sacred relationship, society. By joining society, the individual becomes a *social entity* and must now express respect and honor to all those they encounter in the social milieu. In this way, the individual protects and honors their family's name. Finally, the individual must respect *social norms* and *laws* as they have been created to protect people and societies from falling into chaos.

The previous discussions were a brief introduction to the Far Eastern traditions. Judaism, Christianity, and Islam are no different in that they argue many of the same philosophies of life, but they present these philosophies in other ways or put them in separate containers. Let us begin.

1

Judaism

The Story of Moses

Moses is to the Old Testament as Jesus is to the New Testament. They both play a central role in each of the books, and they both tell us what it means to be human in their own unique way.

The Old Testament took about a thousand years to be put together, and it was written by various people, most of whom are unknown.[1] The folks who have put these books together fall into four groups: the *Elohist*, the *Yahwist*, the *Deuteronomist*, and the *Priestly*.

We encounter the same problem with Moses as we do with the figure of Jesus. It is unclear whether these two figures had a factual historical existence. For example, there is a figure in ancient Syria named Mises, whose story is the same as Moses.[2] In fact, with close observation, you may conclude that Moses's story is no different from the stories of Gilgamesh, the Buddha, Mahavira, and many other similar sages and prophets.

The story is as follows.

The Pharaoh receives a prophecy in a dream that a child will be born who will initiate a Hebrew uprising—a powerful revolution that will topple Pharaoh's kingdom. So troubling is the Pharaoh's dream and its message that he orders all newborn males to be killed. Hearing this, Moses's mother puts Moses in a small basket in a river and faithfully lets the water carry the basket to a safe place. He is abandoned by his true parents and picked up by

---

1. Coogan, *Old Testament*.
2. Brooten, *Women Leaders in the Ancient Synagogue*.

Pharaoh's sister. Moses was always under the impression that this woman was his real, biological mother.

The first message in the story is that, as children, we are all like Moses in assuming that we have immortality in our blood and greatness in our veins. That we know who and what we are. We can trust that our parents will guide us towards understanding and wisdom. This is the arrogance of youth. An arrogance because we haven't yet been tested by the complicated events that life puts before us. All young people have the same hopes and dreams as Moses: in that, we're going to be the next great artist or a revolutionary politician or have a perfect marriage and perfect children. Then, suddenly, tragedy hits, and we realize that we are not who we imagined ourselves to be.

This assumed identity is false in another way. The differences between beggars and kings are accidental, as we did nothing to earn whatever poverties or privileges we have in our lives. Had we been given different parents or been born into other cities, or at a different time in history, our entire lives would be different. We didn't decide on our parents, culture or ethnicity, birthplace, or personality, yet we take these qualities into our identity. Because of this, whenever we begin to ask difficult questions about our identity, we are abandoned by our parents and whatever identities our parents have given us. Parents can provide a home for our bodies but cannot offer our identity or soul.

The story of Moses begins with a man who lives with an unexamined and untested identity, hopes, and ambitions. If you've ever seen the movie *The Matrix*, it says, "Human beings are grown; they're no longer born."[3] Moses, at least initially, is a man who is grown but not yet born.

Tragedy hits Moses one day in his middle age, when he kills an Egyptian soldier and the Pharaoh, who Moses assumed cared for him, sentences him to exile. He is no longer in the garden of Eden. Moses has questions that have set his heart ablaze. His desert life begins because no one has the power to nourish the yearnings of his heart and answer the inquiries of his mind. Moses realizes that he is not what he thought himself to be. Even when he finds out who his true mother is, he's not satisfied. He wants to know his true identity, the identity that is unrelated to space and time.

Like the Buddha, he walks away from his kingdom and distances himself from the people who helped raise him and protect him from harm. He walks away from his biological mother, a woman who longed to be held by

3. Wachowski and Wachowski, *Matrix*.

her son. His physical presence in the desert is a symbol of his psychological state. The desert is where he asks questions and has no idea where to get the answers. He marries, but he's unhappy; he has children, but he's sad; and eventually he realizes that there's something inside him that says, "None of this stuff makes you who you are. You have the Bird of Paradise inside you. Go see if you can find this Bird." This is the God within that Moses is looking for. The story concludes when Moses sees God in the form of a burning bush. At this stage, he starts a new journey, freeing his people. He's no longer an accidental human being, and he's no longer a father or a son or a husband. Moses's journey to God tells us what has to be lost for a person to realize what it truly means to be human. It is through him that Israel and Judaism are born.

What is the relationship between Moses and Judaism?

The traditions that follow the heroes, or prophets, are never as exciting or profound as the heroes themselves. What exactly makes Moses rebel, go on his journey, and then blossom the Spirit of God within? The people who follow Moses try to copy what he did and try their best to protect what Moses had done, but eventually the tradition changes Moses's message. This happens to all of these fountainheads. For example, fourteen or fifteen of the twenty-seven books of the New Testament were written by Paul, who says some beautiful things but never saw Jesus, and never had a relationship with him in person. Paul was never tested by the force of Jesus's personality and his teaching. Christianity is more a reflection of Paul's interpretations of his vision and emotions than of Jesus Christ. The same things happen in every tradition. Buddha never talked about gods, paradise, or hell, but those who came after him tell us of the existence of many compassionate and wrathful deities. The Buddha himself never spoke of such things.

What usually happens is that the hero, like a magnet, attracts lots of people for all the right reasons. Everyone desires to LIVE. And they do so, at least for a short while, through the hero. And when this magnet or hero goes away, the followers assume that they understand who the hero was and what his message entailed. They make commentary on the hero, then there's a commentary on the commentary, and then you have a tradition.

There is a story that comes from the Middle East.[4] Usually, you take a gift when you're invited to someone's house in the Middle East. In this

---

4. Aflaki, *Rumi and His Friends*.

story, the guest brings a duck. Right in front of the guest, the host grabs the duck, twists its neck and kills it, defeathers it, and quickly makes duck soup. And then all of the people sit and have soup. It's real duck soup!

The following day, a stranger comes to the door and says, "I'm the friend of that guy who brought you the duck, and I was told that you have some soup." Middle Easterners are very hospitable people, so he is invited in and given duck soup. Day after day, strangers come and say, "I'm the friend of the friend of the friend who brought you the duck." The man offers all of the soup, but after a while, he says to himself, "This is ridiculous. I don't even know who these people are, yet I have to give them food? I need to put a stop to this." Another guest knocks on the door and says, "I'm the friend of the friend of the friend of the friend who brought you the duck." And the host places a bowl of soup before this man, who takes a spoonful and says, "Wait, this is only warm water." And the host says, "This is the soup of the soup of the soup of the soup." This is what happens to the heroes. Followers ultimately turn them into warm water with no real substance.

We need to understand that Jesus spoke Aramaic, but the New Testament was first written in Coptic, then Greek, Latin, German, and English.[5] And you should be aware that so many things are lost in translation, which makes what we read today the soup of the soup of the soup. The traditions can never covey the passion inside people like Moses and Jesus and the Buddha and Gilgamesh. Do you think that when people today talk about Malcolm X they understand how this man overcame the prison environment and the intoxication of power given to him by Elijah Muhammad? What makes someone like Moses or Jesus just walk away from their life? Why does someone like the Buddha just walk away from a marriage? Do you think these people wake up and say, "I'm walking away"? This is not a single vision—this conflict lives inside them for many years, and then all of a sudden, it erupts. They're depressed, confused, and angry. One day they're good, and the next day they're wrong. They live in this chaotic tornado for years, and then they explode. And all that we see, as the audience, is the explosion. We don't see all of the conflicting emotions inside them.

The disciples, and especially the people who come after the disciples, have none of this. They're poor copies of the real thing. They hear something that sounds nice, store it in their memory, and then regurgitate it like a good parrot with little understanding, and then all of a sudden you have a tradition. They're the soup of the soup of the soup. People like Malcolm

---

5. Ehrman, *Lost Christianities*.

X, Moses, Jesus, and the Buddha are nomads because they have no resting place. Unlike us, they are not guided by tradition. They are living organisms that are guided by the wisdom that is within them. The moment an idea becomes a tradition, it lives in a container with a tightly closed lid. It no longer flows freely and has little life to it. Unless, of course, someone comes and breaks open the cage. Once the cage is broken open, life can flow and live again.

What are the main differences between Moses and Jesus?

The first difference is the personalities of Moses and Jesus, as Moses was very much extroverted and Jesus was very much introverted. But the historical context is also important. The Hebrews in the time of Pharaoh were struggling with their physical life, and they needed a leader like Moses who would help them with their social and political problems.[6] Though in the time of Jesus the Romans still crucified the Hebrews, the Jewish leaders, such as the Pharisees and the Sadducees, had made a deal with the Romans, so they at least had their sections of towns and synagogues where life could go on uninterruptedly. Because of the social and historical differences, the message of Moses is primarily grounded in social and political justice, whereas the message of Jesus is more spiritual.

To put this another way, imagine someone comes your way and says, "I want to understand the meaning of life." And you ask him, "Well, where are you living?" and he says, "In my car." So you say, "Listen. That question is excellent, but right now go somewhere, find a job, save some money, and get yourself an apartment. Once your physical life is set, then you can ask difficult questions." Moses is all about using spiritual ideas to make sure that your physical life is in order because otherwise the questions of physical life will overshadow and swallow the questions of spiritual life. But once physical life is set, you enter into the world of Jesus, which says, "Your physical life is important, but once you get fed up with the physical life, you need an antidote. You need a different force and a different set of ideas to remedy this discontent." Jesus doesn't argue that you need to destroy your physical life or leave your husband or your wife or family. You need to just step into this other inner world for a while. Let's call it "Jesus World," which is about introversion, all about weeping, crying, praying, and intense emotions that disrupt physical life. And, though it's difficult to juggle these two

---

6. Magness, *Stone and Dung*.

worlds, once you become proficient in the world of Jesus, then you can step back into the world of Moses and appreciate your husband or your wife for the person that they are.

There is no difference between the inner journey of Moses and Jesus, but their messages apply to different social and political environments.[7] Suppose you suffer from difficulties in the physical and social world. Like if you have issues with your parents or a toothache, big questions disappear. Moses is about making sure the social world is stable enough so that you can ask difficult questions. When you don't have a toothache, you can attend to more critical questions, symbolized by the predominantly spiritual and esoteric message of Jesus.

Moses and Jesus complement one another. You first need to take algebra before enrolling in calculus. Moses is like a prerequisite to Jesus, in the way that a good physical life is a prerequisite to a good spiritual life.

What is the difference between Judaism and other religions?

All these religious traditions are saying the same thing. In Hinduism, we are born into *Maya*, the ocean of fantasies we create for ourselves. In Buddhism, we are born in ignorance, in not knowing and blindly walking around, hoping that we will get something right. The container looks a little different, but the content is the same.

Imagine you have coffee. Today it's in this cup, tomorrow it's in a different cup, and the next day it's in yet in another cup. And the funny thing is, people begin to fight and say, "You know, the coffee that's in the brown cup tastes the best." But the truth is, if you were to go to a shop that had all different shapes and colors of cups but they all had the same coffee, the coffee would taste the same. If you're fair, honest, and sincere, you would realize that it is the same coffee. But that takes much courage because your ego has to be removed. You have to say, "It is the same coffee, but poured into different containers."

The Garden of Eden

In Judaism, God is the creator of everything. But there is something profoundly special about the human being, as we hold the Breath of God inside

---

7. Shah, *Sufis*.

us. In the Old Testament, no other animal or entity is a suitable container for the Spirit of God, only the human being.[8] Humans live in the garden of Eden, where nothing ever grows old, nothing ever dies, and we don't need to work for anything. Everything is given to us freely, but there is only one problem. God is lonely in the Old Testament. God desires to see himself and feel himself in all shapes and forms. So in the biblical tradition God creates this entity called Adam, which means "dust" or "flesh."[9]

There are two creation stories in the Old Testament, and in the first story Adam walks around and does whatever he wants to do, but God one day comes to him, gazes upon him, and sees that he is miserable. In monotheism, God is all-good, all-knowing, all-perfect, and all-powerful, and yet out of God, who creates nothing but perfection, comes an imperfection named Adam. How could Adam get bored? Many of us have written uninspiring essays that have bored us. Many of us have watched movies that bored us. Many of us have been in relationships that have ultimately bored us. Many of us have sat in classrooms that have bored us. Many of us have even lived lives that have bored us. There is only one outcome for anything that goes back to the flesh: boredom and discontentment.

Seeing how bored the dark, or masculine, force is, how disgusting Adam becomes by living through his physical, fleshy senses, God puts Adam to sleep, takes a rib, turns it into a woman, but does not breathe his Spirit into the woman. Do you know why? Because women and God are the same. They are equal. There is a second creation story in Genesis, in which Adam and his wife, here called Lilith, are created at the same time. However, in both stories, God says to them, and I am paraphrasing, "In this garden, there are a thousand trees. Nine-hundred-and-ninety-nine of these trees are the Trees of Life. Whatever fruits they bear, eat, and have a great time—just a warning: there's one tree, over there; it's the Tree of Death. Don't approach it. It's no good for you." Strangely enough, however, Adam and his wife become interested in the very thing that God warned them against. There is something about us that is curious, that desires perfection and beauty. This desire for perfection condemns us to revolt, against ourselves, against society, and against anyone or anything mediocre and boring.

---

8. Collins and Harlowe, *Eerdmans Dictionary of Early Judaism*.
9. Vanderkam, *Introduction to Early Judaism*.

So there are two parts of us. One is called Eve, which means "life."[10] It is the Utnapishtim or the "life-giver" inside us. The other part is Adam, which means a physical container. Hence, five senses belong to Adam, and another five senses belong to Eve, who desires to experience things divine. If you want your body to come to life and not suffer from boredom in the way that Adam was bored, then make sure that it is governed by your soul, not the other way around.

This is the wisdom that we are given in the Old Testament. In life, it is always Adam, your body, that controls your soul. It's always the fear of money that prevents your creativity. Even if you want to write a creative essay, the fear of a grade, your future, your social standing will put a leash around your neck and say, "The instructor says, 'Double-spaced, font size 12.'"

For those of you who want to know what the garden of Eden is, talk with your work colleagues or your family about such issues as education or relationship, and they will always refer you to a book or a set of inspiring but untested ideas or concepts that have been spoken or written by people they have never met. They will tell you the dos and the don'ts, the rights and wrongs, what is ethical or unethical, what it means to be this and what it means to be that. We have no idea who wrote these books that give us the rights and the wrongs of life. These are the Trees of Life, and all we know is that if we don't obey these things, we get punished.

Yet, for those who are worthy or ready, something exciting happens. Somewhere, somehow, this entity walks into our life. It's the serpent from the Epic of Gilgamesh; it's the snake that lives in the story of Azusa from certain parts of Africa. It's this thing that sheds its skin every year because snakes do something well. They renew themselves. Whatever is old, they get rid of it—all of it—every single year. Without this, the old skin would suffocate and kill them, and it's an excruciating process for serpents. In this garden of Eden, the snake, known symbolically to have profound healing qualities, does not talk to Adam because Adam is the masculine part of us. Keep in mind that you can also be a woman and be governed by Adam. Adam is the physical or dense part of us that's about control, power, security—the tangibles of life, the things you see, hear, touch, smell, and taste. This Adam part has become even more dominant after the nineteenth century. Almost every goal in life, such as happiness, success, and education, is defined by numbers, by tangibles.

10. Vanderkam, *Introduction to Early Judaism*.

Instead, the serpent looks at Eve, this creative part of us, and tempts her. A part of us has lived in this cage but desires to sing and fly.

The serpent says to Eve, "Do you know what you've always wanted?"

And Eve says, "What?"

"Didn't you always want spiritual power?"

"Yes."

"Didn't you always want wisdom?"

"Yes."

After all, you don't read books because they're fun. You read books because you want perspectives. You want to be like God, who can see all the different facets of life. You want to have access to all these different windows, and through these windows you can live through Eve, through the creative and original part of you.

The serpent tells Eve, "That tree over there will give you this knowledge of good and evil. What you want on the inside is not just to be wise. On the inside, you know that *you* are God! This tree will give you the power to claim it! You can walk as God down here. But for that to happen, once you eat this fruit, this fruit will give birth to this thing called conscience, and once conscience gives you awareness, awareness will birth conflict to the point where you can no longer go back to your old life. And when God comes down and asks, 'Where are you?' you will hide parts of yourself because not even God is worthy to know what you know."

In Judaism, we are created to be disobedient! And you don't need Satan—this is who we are! We like running red lights! We enjoy lying! We love cheating! *They bring us to life.* We hate our bosses and discipline because these things cage the spirit within, and the Old Testament tells us how to revolt in the right ways for the right reasons.

And so the serpent convinces Eve, and Eve convinces the body, Adam. "You know the tree that God said, 'Never go near'? That's the tree we need to go to." The body, the container that holds Eve within, very nicely takes Eve to the tree. Eve takes this fruit, puts it in the mouth of Adam, and God says, "Since you did the exact opposite of what I told you, you're both expelled." This story tells us that living down here, outside of the garden of Eden, will be problematic because now you're going to have to work to get everything that was once given freely. Now, you have to develop your rights and wrongs and ethical codes.

The Judaic perspective about the human condition is that for all of us there comes the point in our life where we say, "I don't belong here. This is not my home." How you remember and why you suddenly feel this way are not clear. But when you do remember and feel this way, it seems that Eve comes through. She no longer whispers but screams, "*What are you doing with yourself and your life?*" We never know what or who the serpent will be or how the snake gets through the thick gates of this enormous castle that we create with our physical life. Regardless of all the desires, traumas, passions, and habits, somehow, the serpent enters our lives, finds the creative part of us, and whispers or screams into our ears. Then we wake up, even if it is for a few moments.

> *Why are Adam and Eve kicked out of the garden of Eden? In other words, the serpent gave them freedom, opened the birdcage, and allowed them to sing and fly freely. Were they able to do that beforehand?*

When you have everything, you can't appreciate it. When you lose those things, then the longing, the yearning, the prayer, the contemplation, the reflection, the sadness, and the sorrow begins. These tremendous emotions only come through loss. In this loss, there is wealth, unlike what the modern world and modern people know. In the contemporary world, sadness and depression are viewed and experienced as bad things. Our task is to understand this loss, become intimate with it, learn from it, and grow. Not to get rid of it.

Since all of us are in exile and have been tossed out of the garden of Eden, metaphorically speaking, Judaism tells us that life will be complicated. And just like Buddhism or Hinduism, Judaism tells us that there are ways to restore our lives. In Judaism, this restoration takes place through observing the Ten Commandments.

The Ten Commandments

The Ten Commandments are, according to this tradition, how we overcome our homelessness as a result of expulsion from paradise.[11] However, keep in mind that no one has a monopoly or authority over religious ideas. Ultimately, the more perspectives you have, the more creative you can be with religious ideas and concepts. And they will make your life more

---

11. Charlesworth, *Old Testament Pseudepigrapha*.

meaningful. For example, sit and think, "What exactly is stealing? What is physical stealing? What is emotional stealing? What is intellectual stealing? What is *spiritual* stealing?" Are you stealing when you come to class and go with your friends to a coffee shop and say, "My professor said that Plato said this and Plato said that, or Jesus said this and Jesus said that," if you have no accurate understanding of what your professor said? Do you steal when you simply quote Moses or Jesus to prove a point you are making? Our job is to use the Ten Commandments to make different areas of life more meaningful.

1: I am the Lord your God, and you shall have no other gods before me.

The First Commandment is about henotheism, which means the worship of one God without denying the existence of other gods. There is God, Yahweh, but there are also different deities beneath Yahweh. Worship and respect these other deities but know that they are there because of one God. To put it another way, the idea of beauty is housed in Venus in the Greek tradition, or Ishtar in the Epic of Gilgamesh, or the world of ideas in the Platonic tradition. There is one beauty in paradise, and all the things we see down here are just shadows. Dimmer versions of that beauty.

If we want to transcend our physical lives and move beyond worshipping these lesser deities, we must overcome them. We must remember that these lesser gods exist because of Yahweh. It is he who fuels them and gives them life. It's like praying before eating. You say, "Thank you, God, for giving me this delicious food." What you are saying is, "Whatever I have down here has been given to me by God, whose name is Yahweh." The magic in this is profound. Next time you have any power to do anything, ask yourself how you can do what you are doing. And if you happen to be a follower of the First Commandment, you understand that this power has been given to you by Yahweh himself.

The First Commandment is how we can baptize life down here and claim ownership of absolutely nothing. Everything you have down here is a gift from Yahweh. Worship education, worship your car, worship your husband or wife, but know that all these things are ultimately given to you by God himself. It's like having an orange and using a knife to cut the skin to get to the fruit. The Ten Commandments are like a knife, and once you get to the fruit, the skin is thrown away. When you see the physical world as a gift from Yahweh, then the physical world is no longer just a shadow or a place of corruption. It's a place that reminds you of Yahweh.

If someone asks, "Who exactly is Yahweh? What exactly do you worship?" you enter the Second Commandment.

2: You shall not make any images of God.

The Second Commandment tells us that we cannot speak or even think of Yahweh because he is beyond our senses, thoughts, and imaginations. All we can do is appreciate our life down here because, ultimately, it's being fueled by him. Good or bad, *everything* has been given to us by Yahweh himself. There is no room for complaint. This is a very difficult commandment to follow because it's like going to someone and saying, "I love you, and I want to be with you, but I know you're a living human being who is always changing. If I come home and you're not there, it's okay, but I want to thank you for the moments you have given me." This is so difficult because after spending time with things, psychological narratives are created, and attachment and expectations are born. Yet Judaism argues that life is an environment where events will happen without our consent. You have to be able to summon up the courage to embrace life in any form that comes to you, regardless of your expectations.

Life and God are these winged creatures that like to fly, to be spontaneous, and when you put a bird in a cage, its wings become useless. The Second Commandment argues that when you make an image of anything, you clip its wings, and the moment you clip its wings and box it up, it ceases to be a bird or God or life. Yet human beings, made of flesh and bone, demand security from the physical world. This security is connected to the skin of life, the Adam part of humans. But human beings are also made of light, of spirit, and the task of the Second Commandment is not to make physical images of the spiritual part of life. This puts us in a very uncomfortable position because we can no longer have any expectations from life.

After all, expectations put life into a cage. You can apply to UC Berkeley; you may or many not get accepted. Either way, you have to be okay. You can get married, but whether it lasts or ends in divorce, you have to somehow make peace with it, because though our physical expectations create judgments, the part of us connected to God must be free from judgments. Judgments are expectations, and expectations are your emotions imposed upon life. You're telling life how to function when it is the other way around.

Life is to be free. In short, we cannot have any mental construction of God, and since life comes out of God, we must allow life to guide us instead of directing the flow of life due to our desires and expectations.

3: You shall not misuse the name of God.

Next, you should never allow the word "God" to roll off of your tongue. You can never speak of it. You can talk about the attributes of God, but never God himself. A man in the Persian world named Khajeh Ansari says, "Sometimes when I sit to pray, I have no idea whom to call in my prayer or what to pray to. After all, God lives inside my heart. He knows exactly what my difficulties are. He knows my longings and my yearnings. I can't pray."[12] To put this way easier to understand, next time you want to eat some good food, look for an inspiring movie to watch, or start a marriage with someone, the source and the root of your inspiration is the longing to come to life. Each physical desire is rooted in our quest for freedom and passion, released from the chains created by our body, the past, and life's basic troubles. No matter what name we give it, everything we do daily is a prayer, a way to come closer to God.

In the First Commandment, there is only Yahweh, and in the Second Commandment, you can never have any mental, emotional, spiritual, or physical images of Yahweh. In the Third Commandment, next time you pray, the truth is that you can't have any idea to whom you are praying. All you know is that you are broken and longing for someone or something to make you feel complete.

4: Keep the Sabbath holy.

The first four commandments are about our journey toward God, toward becoming self-sufficient. With self-sufficiency comes the knowledge that God transcends our reflective abilities, exceeds our ability to make images, and even speak about religion, theology, and spirituality. The nineteenth-century Danish philosopher Soren Kierkegaard said, "All theology is blasphemy."[13] The moment you say, "I'm going to teach or study world

---

12. Attar, *Muslim Saints and Mystics.*
13. *Kierkegaard, Either/Or.*

religions," what you're saying is you can tame God's spirit and passion in language, and you have become Satan. You have blasphemed.

Sabbath means a "resting place." It comes to someone who has realized that God or life or truth is beyond human comprehension or understanding. We can only have access to tiny parts of God but will never be able to see the whole of him, yet everything that happens to us happens because of God. That understanding gives you a resting area. To put this another way, initially, we had lots of fear about the answer to 2+2, but now that we understand that 2+2=4, on a good day or a bad day, sunny day or a rainy day, that understanding is your Sabbath to that equation. In the Jewish tradition, the First, Second, and Third Commandments teach us that you will never understand *any* aspect of life. You have to accept everything that life gives you, and that acceptance and surrendering to that acceptance brings about Sabbath.

Elizabeth Kubler-Ross, interested in dying people, argued that almost all who are nearing death go through similar psychological and intellectual processes.[14] First, they deny that they are dying. The reality is too much for them to handle. Then they will fight that reality because they are angry that they are dying. We want to keep our husbands and wives, we want to keep our jobs, and we want to save our lives, and when we truly realize that we will lose them, depression sets in. Then we begin to bargain: "God, if you give me another week, I'll be good to my kids. If you give me another year, I'll give all my money away." After a while, when the dust settles from this battle, every near-death person will say, "God's will be done. I accept that I have cancer, and I may die in a timely fashion or untimely fashion, but I am okay with death." That knowledge becomes your Sabbath.

Those who may be going through difficulties in life recognize that problems exist only when there is no fundamental understanding. If suddenly you were given a quiz and there was only one question, "What is 3+3?" no one would sweat because you know the answer is 6. It's a mathematical problem, but it doesn't create confusion or fear because you understand the problem and know the answer. In life, if you want to know what the difficulty is and how it came about and what you need to do, go back to the first three commandments. What is it about you that expects life to be different? What makes you think you are in control of anything? Why have you become like a tax collector on the inside, where you go through life demanding that life gives you something in return?

---

14. Kubler-Ross, *On Grief and Grieving*.

Now that we know that no amount of reading books will ever give you access to see the face of God, now that we know that synagogues don't hold the image of God because, unlike the human heart, no place can ever be strong enough or vast enough to hold the Spirit of God, then the only sacred place is the place that you choose to be holy. You will no longer desire to even speak of God. What can we know? Our salvation is in accepting the fact that we'll never reach God, and we'll never know what his intentions are and what he looks like. All you can do is rest and accept that you have no power over anything. Yet all that takes place in your life is God's doing.

The first four commandments are about your spiritual growth and intellectual and emotional maturity, and once the first four have been completed, you can walk into the last six commandments, which are about harmoniously living your physical life.

5: Honor your father and mother.

First, we'll do it the easy way, and then we'll make it a little bit more complicated. There are two forces inside us, and these are our two parents. The masculine—the Adam—demands food, money for rent, pleasure, and entertainment. That's the father. Then there is the mother—Eve—who requires and demands creativity to come to life. You can't be a monk and walk away from physical responsibilities to only concern yourself with spiritual things. Both the physical and the spiritual are important, and they both need to be adequately nourished. Remember, God created the physical body. The spiritual body is the Spirit of God, which is held inside the physical body. Both need to be tended.

But forget all those esoteric, spiritual ideas for now. For those of you who feel that your parents have abandoned you, betrayed you, lied to you, did this to you and that to you, and you've been trying endlessly to figure out why your parents are a certain way, all you need to do is closely study the Fifth Commandment, especially within the context of the other commandments and the entirety of Judaism.

We are condemned to be animals that desire closeness. It's natural, and it's human. A man and a woman don't go toward each other because they both understand each other's soul or even know and acknowledge that they have souls. Their eyes, very organically, say, "That person is beautiful." Like magnets, they go toward one another. How do human beings ultimately connect? How do they eventually communicate these feelings of beauty, especially if there is a good amount of passion? Like God, we use the physical world to express the spiritual passion that awakens in us. Next time you fall in love with someone and you want to physically express this love, it has nothing to do with physicality. It is your soul, your desire for passion, expressing itself to another soul. You are intimate with their soul, their desire to be in touch with beauty. In this scenario, you have two twenty-year-olds who don't understand all the different forces erupting within them and how they affect each other. They don't understand the concepts of beauty, passion, and magnetism. They know they want to be close, and eventually they become. And remember, Eve doesn't care about contracts. Eve doesn't care about discipline. Eve is rebellious. Eve doesn't care about, "What if I get pregnant?" Eve screams, "Passion!"

But all these invisible forces must also respect the physical forces, and when the physical forces come into play, the cycle is delayed, and the woman goes to the man and says, "I think I am pregnant." All of a sudden, there are no longer spiritual entities. These are physical human beings who will suffer doubts. "Am I old enough to be a father or a mother? Am I educated? Do I have money? Do I have housing?" But the most innocent part of us, the part that holds life itself to be sacred, says, "I will do whatever I can to protect my son or my daughter." We see our children as what Jean Jacques Rousseau, the Genevan philosopher, would call the "noble savage," and will do whatever we can to make sure society never corrupts and contaminates them.[15]

But all human beings have a certain capacity. Eventually, the stories that your twenty-five-year-old father or twenty-year-old mother created of marriage, degrees, and grandchildren will fall victim to the limitations we have as humans and as parents. If there is too much social and financial pressure and not enough support, your mom may slowly begin to care for you less, and your dad may slowly detach. But what is honorable about your parents are the stories they initially created and all the effort they put forth into bringing these stories to life: "I will do my best to protect my kids. I will make rent, and I will suffer so that my child, my soul, is protected from society." Your mom is a physical human being, frustrated by a life and a world that seems uncaring and indifferent. She is crucified by her lack of understanding, lack of rest, and lack of Sabbath, and like any other animal, she doesn't know how to deal with pain besides doing things that make the pain go away, even for a moment. You're not going to respect the woman

---

15. Rosseau, *Social Contract*.

who drinks to escape the difficulties of her life. But you will respect the stories that she had about you and motherhood before certain hard realities of life brutalized her. You don't honor your physical parents, who were thrown into the world without any knowledge of how to deal and cope in a world filled with hostile forces and little power to control the forces of life. You have to respect the souls of your parents—the stories, intentions, and pain that live inside them.

6: *Thou shalt not kill.*

There is a book by the Algerian philosopher Albert Camus called *The Plague*.[16] In one scene, a priest goes before the people and says to them, "It is true that everyone around us is dying, but there is a purpose in death. Have faith in God!" There is a doctor in the church, and he hears what this man is saying, and he says, "That is wrong." When the sermon is over, he goes, grabs this priest by the neck, and says, "You need to come to the hospital with me." He forces this priest's head down to gaze into the eyes of a two-month old baby who's screaming because there is so much pain inside him. The doctor asks, "What has this innocent life done to be deserving of being murdered so carelessly by life?" And of course, because he doesn't want to lose face, the priest comes up with all these grand stories of life, but when he leaves the hospital, he knows he's a charlatan, a fake. He goes to the cemetery, and there is this big, gigantic hole. He looks around to make sure no one is watching. He lays flat in the hole, and the bulldozer fills it with gravel in the morning. The priest kills himself because the truth is, we have no idea why such terrible things happen to us.

To put it another way, there is a Persian poem that says, "Oh God, if you want to take my life, take it when I have passion inside of me."[17] When you have a juicer, you put the fruit in and the juice comes from one side, but the rind, the junk, comes from the opposite side. If you're creative, you can put the skin on your face as a mask, you can use it as compost, but most often you trash the rind. And the prayer in this poem is, "If I have any passion inside me, please don't let me get to old age to where my passion is gone, and then kill me. Because that's like living a life without any juice. Let me be at my zenith, at the pinnacle, at the top of Mount Everest. Let me look at all of the cosmos from the top, then have someone push me to my

16. Camus, *Plague*.
17. Helminski, *Love's Ripening*.

death. Because if I come down, I will only have the memories of being alive. And that's not a good way to live."

This commandment is about respecting life. However, should you be forced to take a life, any life, make sure you do not waste what you have destroyed. Make sure that the life that you have taken will taste a different kind of life. A more meaningful and creative life. Don't just kill an animal and just lounge around. That is destroying two lives: yours and the cow's. Take the life of a cow and feed yourself to have a sufficient amount of energy to write a beautiful poem or an inspiring painting. Then you are observing one of the commandments.

7: Thou shalt not commit adultery.

Adultery can be looked at in a variety of different ways. In the most literal sense, we are not the sort of animals that do well in open relationships, at least at this stage of our human evolution. The social, physical, and psychological worlds make us far too insecure about ourselves and our future, which makes us possessive, jealous, and petty in all sorts of ways. Marriage is highly complicated these days, and open relationships for many of us stem from the fact that we are bored and want to spice up our life a little or we have difficulty with commitment for various reasons.

There is another version of adultery that may be too advanced for us but is much more profound and interesting. There is a movie called *Elizabeth*, which came out in 1998.[18] It's about a woman who becomes the queen of England, and because of her England has its golden age and becomes prosperous, wealthy, and stable. This woman, Elizabeth, found a man and was very much in love with him, only to realize that he was already married, so he could no longer be touched or even looked at. She can't bring herself to love another man because she knows that she'd be lying to herself, which a similar to stealing or deceiving yourself. In other words, her conscience says, "You can only be with a man you love, no other. Regardless of how lonely and desperate you may be, you can only satisfy your hunger if there is love." She is in the church in her palace, and her advisor comes in, and she begins to weep. Elizabeth says, looking at a statue of Mary, "Mary had so much power over the hearts of people." And her advisor says, "All human beings desire to be touched by something divine down here." For whatever reason, that clicks and creates an opening inside Elizabeth, and she says, "If

18. Kapur, *Elizabeth*.

I can marry God, that is, if I can have God inside me and be God's bride, I will have no human being in my bed, only God."

In our love affairs with almost everything, the undercurrent is our desire to come to life. And in Judaism, like the Epic of Gilgamesh, Hinduism, and Buddhism, coming to life means having a relationship with the divinity inside. This divinity, God, is the only person with whom we can sleep. Our soul is feminine, and the only person worthy of being intimate with our souls is not a human being but Yahweh himself. Not only is it a love affair, but we want to become like Yahweh. So to keep ourselves from becoming adulterous, the only person with whom we can be intimate is Yahweh. Anyone else is adultery. This means you have to see the divinity in everything you are in a relationship with; otherwise it is considered adultery.

8: Thou shall not steal.

There is a movie from 2005 called *V for Vendetta*.[19] The main character is a revolutionary, and he takes a woman to his underground bunker. He's making her toast with butter, and she asks him, "Where did you get the butter?"

He says, "From the government."

And she says, "You stole?"

He says, "No, heavens no. Stealing is like claiming ownership. I only took the stuff that I needed."

The truth is, our bodies are not ours. Our emotions are not ours. Our reflections are not ours. Do you ever go to these places like Rent-A-Tool? In Judaism, the ultimate owner of everything in life is God. Never claim ownership of anything. There is nothing wrong with wanting comfort or pleasure, but first, know that your body is on rent from God, and your soul is given to you by God, so if you want to have pleasure, ultimately, it needs to go back to God. It can't be *your* pleasure—it needs to be baptized.

We all want private ownership over our experiences and emotions. All religious traditions tell us that we are not our bodies. For example, we all have experiences with close relationships, whether friends or family or otherwise. These relationships create experiences, and these experiences create emotional reactions. But if it are not our body, this emotion comes and then it goes. It has to disappear. We cannot hang onto the memory and create history because it doesn't belong to us. It belongs to the moment, but now that the moment has left, it's finished. This commandment is about

---

19. McTeigue, *V for Vendetta*.

fixing the parts of us that forget to whom this place belongs and how life was given to us.

Stealing is like plagiarism. It is not yours, but because you are lazy or untalented or can't manage your time correctly, you take from others and claim it as your own. It could be argued that almost all aspects of our lives have been plagiarized. That is stealing. There is no Sabbath, no resting place in stealing. There is no real understanding when you steal something and claim it as your own. It is only through observing the first four commandments that stealing ceases to exist.

9: Thou shalt not lie.

Lying is the way that we survive, both socially and psychologically. We have to lie to society, for it will only accept you if you lie to it. If your instructor asks you if your classes are engaging, raise your hand and say, "Yes, it's most interesting," because you need the grade. Even to ourselves, every time we hear a voice that says, "You're not living life fully," we drown the voice out because often being honest with ourselves is too devastating.

An Armenian philosopher named G.I. Gurdjieff repeatedly said that as long as human beings don't know themselves, they have no choice but to lie.[20] How can you profess to love someone when you don't know yourself? How can you say that you are happy when you don't know yourself? How can you claim to be religious, a student, or an artist when you don't know yourself? In this way, he argued that all speech or expression without self-knowledge is a lie.

Remember, in Judaism, there are two forces inside us. If the physical force, your body, is hungry, don't lie to it. Feed it some food. And if the second force, your spirit, decides to voice itself, allow it to. Don't dismiss these parts. Being honest with yourself is much more complex than being honest with other people. To be honest with oneself is not to mistake assumptions for facts because that would be a lie. Never be completely honest with people, but always be honest with yourself, and don't believe the lies that you tell society or the ones that society tells you. No one needs to know, but just don't lie to yourself. Go home from your classes and work, and say to yourself, "You know, that class and that job are no good," because then you are honest with the part of you that is most worthy of your honesty.

---

20. Ouspenski, *In Search of the Miraculous*.

Judaism

10. Thou shalt not covet.

The first four commandments are spiritual, in the sense that they're about our relationship to God, and Fifth through Ninth Commandments are physical, in the sense that they're about our relationship to society. But the last commandment is psychological, in that it's about our relationship with ourselves. Everybody in society has something interesting to offer us that we don't have. If you are a married man or a woman, there will always be someone who has features or qualities that your companion doesn't have. One of the ways that you silence this temptation is to breathe the spiritual commandments into physical commandments and inwardly become content with what God has given you. Your wife or husband may not be as intellectual, exciting, or spiritual as you want them to be, but remember, all things in Judaism are given to us by God. In this way, each of the commandments contains the others. For example, you can't physically, emotionally, intellectually, and spiritually steal from other people and claim them as your own. Prohibiting coveting is a way to protect society, other people, and ourselves.

As a whole, the commandments argue that inside every human being lives an image of God, and ultimately that's what needs to be worshipped. Not the physical being, but the spiritual being inside. And inside every human being, there is this intense desire to come to life, and in Judaism coming to life means blossoming the image of God that lives within.

The Book of Job

Background

Even if you're allergic to religion and the Bible, the book of Job in the Old Testament is beautiful poetry. No one knows who wrote the book of Job and some people argue that it is the oldest book of the Old Testament.[21] But the truth is that the book of Job is not original. Just like the story of Moses, there's another book from the Mesopotamian tradition with a character who functions like Job, but that is unimportant.[22] What is important is that the book of Job is about the problem of evil, or sin, or pain. We are given just a few decades to live, and somehow we have been given this profound,

---

21. Cohen, *From the Maccabees to the Mishnah*.
22. Collins and Harlowe, *Eerdmans Dictionary of Early Judaism*.

fantastic conscience and the responsibility that in our short lifetime, despite all our immature desires, we must also understand the meaning and purpose of existence. Before you die, you have this desire to understand who you are, what you are, the meaning of your life, how to deal with all the burdens and problems of life, and whether God exists. You have to understand this whole game, yet the book of Job says you will never know.

In the Old Testament, God desires to see his own image in people, society, politics, and all aspects of human life. But this image of God can only blossom if the human being is cracked and shattered into pieces. Consider the poem: imagine there is a light bulb and it's lit, and you put this light bulb in a box and close the box. If this light bulb is in a box, you can never see the light. But now break the box in half, and make sure it's cracked open, and all of a sudden all this light comes out. In the book of Job, we see that the only reason human beings were given a heart was for it to be broken. In this brokenness, the human heart begins to see the light that has always lived within but forgotten.

In the book of Job, suffering has a purpose. You may not know what the purpose of it is and you will never understand your pain, but it is alchemy. It is magic. It transforms iron into gold.

The first bet

The story begins with a man named Job, and God loves Job.[23] One day, Satan somehow finds himself in the presence of God. God looks at Satan and says, "Where have you been?" The first thing to note is that God and Satan are very close, and we will see later why this is important. Satan replies, "I was down on this place called Earth." God replied, "Did you see a guy whose name is Job? He is my most faithful, my most favorite servant. He is the image of perfection." Satan laughs at God and says, "Surely you must be mistaken. You know, Job is not as great as you think him to be." God says, "No, you can't find anyone like him on this planet. He is unique." And Satan says, "No. I will show you if you let me." And God says, "Okay."

Job has no idea what's about to happen, because, like us, he does not know what the next moment will bring. We are entirely in the dark, though we assume that we are in control of our own lives and that our will and efforts are enough to control and guide our lives. But the book of Job shows

---

23. Mitchell, *Book of Job*.

Judaism

us everything is done behind closed doors, and we are simply puppets. Things happen to us, and often you cannot understand why.

At the story's beginning, Job has everything you and I want out of life. He has physical security because he has a humongous property, lots of money, lots of animals, and lots of kids. Remember that God says of him, "He is one of my favorite servants. I like him. He is the most righteous. You will find no other person who is more righteous than Job." This means that Job also has emotional security, as he would go to the synagogue and pray and do all the religious rituals properly. Job is a man of strong faith and is therefore a very happy man. If you asked him many questions, he would give you all the correct answers. It's a beautiful life.

To put it another way, imagine that you are Job. You have your health and nice clothes, you have rent money, go to school, and have fun, and your life is meaningful. Then Yahweh looks down and says, "Ah! What a good kid!" Satan comes to God and says, "God, you know that deep down, you want to see your image in this kid. He's not as good as you think him to be." And God says, "What should be done?" Satan replies, "Let me go do a few things to his physical life, and once I shatter him, maybe this light can come out, and this kid can see a different image of himself, and you too can see a different image—of yourself in him." And God says, "You know, if the pain becomes too overwhelming, he will kill himself. Just make sure, whatever you want to do to his life, he doesn't become suicidal." And Satan says, "Yeah, I will make sure."

Our preoccupation for the past millions of years has been physical security. We want to make sure we have a fridge and lots of food in it, that we have next month's rent because this physical security gives us direction and purpose in life. It is an excellent GPS to life. But neither God nor Satan desires that. They both want something different for you, but how do you make someone think? Feel? How do you paralyze the calculator that a person has in this head, theh one that has been socialized, that turns everything into a profit or loss? Something devastating has to happen to overcome our desire for physical and emotional security. Somehow, Job has to find his physical life meaningless to see this light within him.

Satan comes back down to Earth to prove that God is wrong, to show that when Job goes through hardship in physical life, he will turn his back to God and blaspheme. Satan creates an environment where Job's goats, cows, and sheep die, and all of his crops wither away, and he loses all his money. Job has no idea what's happening because he thinks of himself as a good person and undeserving of any calamity. He is religious, and he does the proper rituals and sacrifices and all the signs of a good person.

Put differently so that we can all understand a bit better, he goes to class every night, takes notes, submits all of his work. But there is no real understanding of the course materials. Even though he does everything right, both Job and this student are profoundly egocentric, one of the most significant obstacles in understanding. Job assumes that just because he can live on the surface of life, that is sufficient. But both Yahweh and Satan have had different plans for him.

Job tries to understand, but before he can ever approach what he's experienced, God and Satan do another thing to Job. An environment is created where Job's sons are all killed. With no more money, no more property, and no more sons, Job sits back and says, "What did I do wrong? Why did all of my animals and sons die?" First you have lost your animals. Now you've lost your kids. But it seems Job is thick-skinned. His animals die, and he says, "God gives and God taketh away. It's okay." His kids die—I mean, they are murdered—and you know what he says? "God giveth, and God taketh away." Talk about religion being the opium of the masses!

Mrs. Job, the woman who has gaven birth and spent her life with all these children, watches all of her kids being butchered alive by these thieves, watches all these animals dying and crops being ruined, looks at her husband and says, "How could you worship this God? You do everything for Yahwah, and in the end, this is the way he rewards you? How could you *want* to worship such a God? Curse God!" And Job says, "No, I am not in the mind of God. I have no idea why God does what he does. I have no access to the wisdom of God. Things happen to us for specific reasons." But he says this intellectually, and he doesn't feel or understand what he says.

Keep in mind that Job is one of the chosen people of God. The book of Job illustrates this world in that bad things will happen to all of us and in all of our lives. This means that any soul that comes in a physical body is a chosen person of God. It doesn't matter how good or moral you may be. It doesn't matter how religious or spiritual you may be. Bad things will happen. This is inevitable. In addition, you're not going to understand why things are happening to you. All of us try to be decent, ethical, and kind people, but who can we blame it on when bad things happen? Maybe in heaven somewhere, God looks down and says, "Mediocre life. As long as he has his father, as long as he has his mother, as long as he has food, as long as he has money, he will remain mediocre." Pain and struggle and their overcoming make for a heroic and valuable life.

The profundity of Satan

To understand the book of Job, we need to understand the profundity of Satan. God creates things because he wants to see his image. This is no different from how we choose the books we want to read, the music we want to listen to, and the way we spend time with specific people who have specific temperaments. We choose all of these carefully because we want to see certain parts of ourselves come out. We want these things to speak to our emotions.

It seems that God, despite all of his genius, creates things like the mountains and the seas but still doesn't see his image. Finally, God puts himself inside the human being, and the human being can hold God within. After God creates the human being, He calls all the angels to gather, including Satan. Before Satan falls, his name is Lucifer, which means "the bringer of light."[24] Lucifer brings enlightenment. God asks all the angels to bow to the human being, and no angel challenges God except Lucifer. He tells God, "I am made of fire and light. A human being is made of dust and dirt. Do you want fire, something that illuminates and generates heat, to bow before dirt? Never. My job, as an angel, is only to worship Yahweh, not the human being." Satan is a pure monotheist in that he wants to be in love with God and no other. God looks at him and says, "If you can just exercise some creativity, you can see God inside the human being. Worship the human being because he is Me." And Satan says, "No. I'm not going to do that." In this way, Lucifer falls.

Satan is the serpent in the garden of Eden, in which the garden of Eden represents a human being who lives a comfortable life. In the garden of Eden, we have intellectual answers to all of life's problems. We have scheduled our lives into small compartments. We assume what we will do and how our future will unfold. But Satan knows the human being must fall, and his life must shatter to remember the spark of divinity that exists within him but has been forgotten under an avalanche of human desires and ambitions. And the only way the human being falls is by God allowing this serpent, a creature that symbolizes health and wellness, to enter human life. To destroy human life and tempt him to live an examined life and give

24. Mitchell, *Book of Job*.

birth to conscience to make him feel guilty for what he has become. This is no different from the story of Socrates. Socrates is like a gadfly, like a serpent who stings you and bites you. Then pain follows. In discomfort, you cry, and your tears are like wings. The more you flap your wings, the higher you go. The higher you, the better you can see your life. The better you can see your life, the more you accept it. The more you can accept it, the better you can live it. The garden of Eden, the book of Job, and the story of Socrates are the same stories just written at different times.

But these are not just stories, as there have always been different groups in various societies who play the role of Lucifer or Satan. For whatever reason, like Satan in the book of Job, there are groups of people who are clairvoyant and can see inside the human being, and they have access to worlds that you and I don't. Some of these people do the following. They go and find troubled environments and, for example, go to a person and say, "You need to get married." Now imagine that you have come from a challenging background. You have seen your parents fight all the time, you have seen your father walk away from your mother, or both of your parents have abused you in different shapes and forms. You have also tried being in relationships, only to realize they don't work well, so you never get emotionally involved. With anyone. Now a stranger walks into your life and says, "You're stuck." And you say, "What do you mean 'stuck'?" "You're stuck. The only way for you to progress, the only way to mature or evolve is to get married. You have to force yourself to jump through this hurdle. Otherwise, what's going to happen is this. If you don't overcome your difficulties, you're going to have a child with someone, and your child will have to overcome these things. But for your child to go through this hurdle, he must go through the same experiences that you've gone through. Why don't you do this yourself so that you can give your kid the proper tools that help in overcoming life's difficulties?"

The book of Job shows the limitation of human understanding. Ultimately, philosophy and religion were created because we can't cope and understand life and all the difficulties it makes.

The second bet

Satan goes back to paradise and sits with God, and God says, "Did you see my faithful servant Job? He did not complain, blaspheme, ane never said, 'God is bad' and made a judgment. He said, 'God gives and God taketh away.'" And Satan again laughs at how foolish God can be. He looks at God and says, "You and I know full well that someone who spends his time in the synagogue is not attached to his kids, is not emotionally connected to his wife, and doesn't care much about his animals. He is much more interested in himself, so, of course, when his kids are butchered, he's not going to cry—he accepts this because there is no relationship! And if there is no relationship, there is no emotional connection. And if there is no emotional connection, when the kids go away, there is no grief or feeling of loss or weeping. No one gets broken!"

Satan continues, "You know, since Job is so dense, we're going to threaten him by getting him very close to death itself. Job has a relationship with himself and with his body. Let me go down there, do a couple of things, and you will see that Job is not the man that you thought him to be." And God says, "Fine, as long as you don't kill him, do whatever you want."

You can always replace your car, shoes, or phone should you lose them. Satan in this story is our teacher because he inspires negative experiences that touch things to which we are emotionally attached. When something that has become part of who and what you are is taken away, something you expect life to offer you, we begin to complain and lament. According to the book of Job, transformation takes place only when things to which we are emotionally connected are taken away. You have to be touched most profoundly. You have to be broken! This is the task of Satan!

Job wakes up, and he's in pain. His body has all these sores, and finally, Job has absolutely nothing. Job finally wakes up a little, and he wants to understand. He's confused, angry, and depressed and doesn't know why all this stuff is happening: "I go to the synagogue and pray to God. How could God do such evils to me?"

For the first time in Job's life, he feels something, and what he feels is not pleasant. Job wants to know why God is doing all this stuff to him, and he wants to know why he's in so much pain. You will no longer see Job's wife in the picture, because she no longer needs to come to him and say, "Curse God and die." He begins to curse on his own. For the first time, Job says, "I want to die." For the first time, he says, "Why didn't the Earth open up to swallow me?" For the first time, he says, "Why didn't the milk in my mother's breast turn to poison?" This is not a happy man anymore who accepts God's will. He wants to know why God has done this to him.

Morality and ethics in the book of Job

The book of Job needs to be understood within the context of Deuteronomy, Leviticus, and the other Wisdom books of the Old Testament. According to these books, God will never do anything evil to someone good. God will never do something good to someone evil. We imagine that by going to school, paying our taxes, buying groceries for our parents, and doing all this excellent stuff, God will look down and protect us and our life and my family. That is the foundation of *every* morality: do good, and good things will come to you. To understand the psychology of Job, you have to understand that, as the beginning of the book shows, he has never done anything wrong. But God and Satan, according to the book of Job, don't care how well you look in the eyes of people or society.

To look at it from an even more rational or impersonal perspective, life doesn't find life valuable. It destroys it. For example, in 2003 there was an earthquake in a city in Iran called Bam, and about thirty thousand people died in one minute. Ever since human beings have been around, we have been engaged in warfare. Even we don't find life valuable. We send kids out there to fight. We see impoverished people on the streets every day, dismiss them, and look the other way. Earthquakes, famines, and floods are all indications that life doesn't find life valuable. It only has one function: it destroys, it creates. It destroys, it creates. You can't impose human morality onto life. The book of Job shows us that life, or God, doesn't work that way.

But like all of us, Job doesn't understand this and wants to know, "I have been good all of my life. Why is this happening to me?" Who among us doesn't think we are intelligent, wise, intuitive, and insightful? All of us suffer from the same arrogance. Imagine you were to read many books. What for? You're going to gain what, precisely, from reading books and taking notes? You read books to what—to inflate your ego some more? You will learn *nothing* by reading, writing, and thinking. That is the wisdom from the book of Job. You will get nothing from marriage, nothing from having children, nothing from that which exists outside of you. All the wisdom that you and I accumulate is counterfeit because when we are tested, we fall apart.

From this point on, Satan is no longer in the picture. The task of Satan in the book of Job is simple. He sets certain things in motion, then lets things play out. Let the human being suffer, and in the end, hopefully, he will understand. If you have been broken, you demand justice and demand to know why this has happened to you.

Judaism

Job's friends: Eliphaz, Bildad, Zophar, and Elihu

In the book's third part, three friends named Eliphaz, Bildad, and Zophar hear of the calamities that have befallen Job. They go to him and tell him, "There is a reason why all of this stuff is happening to you," and they try to convince him that bad things happen to people because God sees them as bad and therefore punishes them. It is God's will that he should suffer. But Job continues to claim his innocence. "But I have been righteous. I am sinless. I am wise and intuitive and religious and spiritual, and I can't understand why God is doing this to me."

There comes the point in the book where Job raises his hand, clenches his fist, looks at the heavens, and says to God, "If I have sinned, show me." This is like those of us who are in relationships when our companions are doing things that hurt us, and we say, "I have done nothing but good to and for them; they have no right doing this to me!" But we have no idea what gets broken inside the human heart. We have no idea why people become discontent and unhappy. You may think it's about you, but it's not. Every once in a while, you realize that it doesn't matter what you and I do for our companions. Because we are born in sin, in the cradle of discontent, we are born to grieve, which means we are born to be broken and remain broken and spend all of our lives trying to mend our hearts. But it can never be done. Job, like the rest of us, demands justice: "All of my life I have done good, and the only thing I get back is pain, and I want to know why." Every time a friend tries to convince Job of the reasons why these awful things have been happening to him, Job replies, "I am sinless. I am righteous."

There is a fourth friend at the end of the book, named Elihu. Just like the German philosopher Immanuel Kant, Elihu argues that we are enormously complicated, and because of this, we can never honestly know our intentions.[25] To put this another way, in the ancient Greek world, the chief deity was Zeus.[26] Zeus is the god of lightning, and according to the Greek tradition, lightning occurs when Zeus becomes angry. The Greeks argue that because anger is a judgment, only Zeus, not the human being, has the authority to become angry at anything. When you and I have emotional outbursts, what we're saying is, "I understand the inner world of this situation. I understand how this experience is going to change me twenty years from now." In other words, every judgment allows you to assume that you

---

25. Kant, *Observations*.
26. Apollodorus and Hard, *Library of Greek Mythology*.

are all-knowing like God, which gives you the power to deem something as good and evil, right and wrong. Elihu tells Job, "Why do you keep saying that you are sinless and righteous? Isn't it ultimately true that God is the only person who has access to the human heart?"

If you want to enjoy this life, though it is filled with suffering, misery, and betrayals, in the first stage of suffering, like Job, you tear your robe and say, "What is happening to me?" In the second stage, you grieve and say, "I want to die." In the third stage, you'll find that all your friends who can no longer bear to see you suffering come to you and try to explain things to you, and you realize there is a difference between feeling and thinking. His friends try to make Job understand intellectually why he deserves suffering. But Job has a tornado on the inside. He feels too much, and so he says, "You guys have no idea what you're talking about! Emotions go beyond rationality!" And then, finally, the story concludes by showing us how Job, after all this suffering, sees himself in life and God.

Conclusion

In the end, God appears to Job—not physically, of course—looks at Job, and says, "You foolish man. All you human beings know how to do is to complain. Where were you when I made the stars, the heavens, the sun? What do you know about anything? Why can't you just accept the things that are given to you? Why do you have to claim them to be good or bad, right or wrong? Why can't you live your life the best you can?"

For the first time, Job begins to realize his utter insignificance. He realizes that he can't know anything and will never learn anything. His intellect, despite being fantastic machinery, will never have access to the mind of God. At the end of the book, this man gets broken. He tries to understand why life is so lousy, and ultimately he kneels, grabs some dirt, pours it over his head, and says, "Dust on my head." The man who assumed himself sinless gets baptized by brokenness for the first time. Like Jesus in the garden of Gethsemane, Job says, "Thy will be done. You're in charge. I will accept what is put on my plate. I will never, ever, ever challenge you." And ultimately, that's how our position should be in life. We have no idea why things happen the way they do. For those who want to understand something, read the book of Job. Almost every one of us, metaphorically, is a Job, and now, for the first time, Job can accept all the things that will happen to him.

Judaism

The point of the story of Job is that nobody knows what is going on. The best thing you can do is be okay with life breaking you and shattering you into pieces. Metaphorically kneel, bow, grab some dirt or dust, and pour it over your head to signify that you are lower than dirt. There is no way you can understand *anything* about this life. Let life walk on you, because the most incredible blessing any human being can have in life is to be the ground upon which God walks. That is when Job submits: "I cannot understand life. I will simply accept what it offers me." And when he finally submits and surrenders, God gives him fifty thousand cows, much property, and many daughters. It seems that when you no longer want to understand, when you no longer have any desires, when you have genuinely embraced life regardless of how lousy it may be at times, life plays another trick on you. It gives you everything you have ever wanted, but you are forced into a stage where you no longer want or need them. It's messed up. You pursue, and life takes everything away; you give up, and life gives you everything. It just doesn't make any sense.

One of the best accounts of the book of Job for us modern people is in a book with nearly a thousand pages called *Daughter of Fire*.[27] It's about a woman who assumes that she can learn and never complains. She had been a theosophist, so she thought she had known the ways of God and learned the way of God. She had been around other teachers, so she had assumed she knew how teaching and learning work. So she goes to India, and she looks at this man and says, "I am here because I want to know God." And all that this man, Bhai Sahib, does is laugh and say, "Really?" And the woman says, "Yes." And then he begins to slowly, emotionally and intellectually, go inside this woman and destroy all the metaphorical and symbolic children that she has, which are her ideas, beliefs, dreams, expectations, and false assumptions about anything and everything she assumed to know.

This book suggests that if you want to learn anything worth learning, it can't be done through books. It can't be done by going to school. If you want to know how much power you have, pay attention to those moments in life when you're completely broken and depressed. When, metaphorically speaking, your back bends and your knees are broken, you will see that you have no power at all over life. You cry and moan and scream, and in the end, this brokenness is what makes you religious. After this, you will accept, but not before a good fight. This last part in the book of Job is the signature of humility, which is what brokenness does. Imagine if there

---

27. Tweedie, *Daughter of Fire*.

was no Satan and there was only God, and there were only our egos telling us how great and attractive we are, how intelligent and insightful we are, and we were never to be tested. Most of us, lucky for us, get tested by little things. Job is tested not by physical things, but his soul is tested and crucified, and all the arrogance that lived inside him oozes out. Through Satan, Job is purified.

For those going through difficult times, you should ask for more difficulties to come your way until emotionally, intellectually, and spiritually, there is no movement from you. You get into this fetal position and cry, and then God will come. That's the book of Job—the profundity of Satan.

2

CHRISTIANITY

WE DON'T KNOW IF Jesus existed. Some say Jesus was a mythical figure, and some say that this man walked the Earth.[1] But it doesn't matter who this man was, real or mythical, and people wrote many inspiring books about this figure. Many of these stories are in the New Testament, the second part of the Bible. The New Testament is a collection of twenty-seven books, fourteen of which are letters written by St. Paul. Four of these books contain stories of Jesus Christ, called "gospels." We don't know the gospels' authors, but these books include fantastic stories about human capacity and potential. There are about forty gospels in total, all giving us different perspectives on who and what this man was and what he did. Some books express portray man to be very mean-spirited. Some books offer a more generous account of Jesus. We'll first talk about the canonized version of Jesus Christ, the stories in the Bible, and then we'll talk about the gospels of which the church disapproved.[2]

The history of the texts themselves is fascinating. For example, if today you were asked who Jesus Christ is, you would probably say, "He had a mother named Mary who was a virgin. God spoke to Mary, then she became pregnant, and later Jesus was born." But the truth is, two thousand years ago very few people knew how to read or write, and monasteries were lucky to have a single book.[3] Usually, what happened is that five villages shared one book—say, for example, the Gospel of Mark, which doesn't

1. Ehrman, *Lost Christianities*.
2. Metzger, *Canon of the New Testament*.
3. Harrington, *What Are They Saying about Mark?*

contain any of this information. And then, one hundred miles away, there is another village, and in this village they have no idea who Mark is because the only book they have is the Gospel of Matthew. Then you walk another hundred miles, and the people in that village have no idea who Mark or Matthew is because they only have access to the Gospel of Philip, or Judas, or Nicodemus, for example. After the fifteenth century, with the invention of the printing press in Germany, we have publications and the brand new professions of reading and writing. In the twenty-first century, you can go to Amazon and buy the Old and New Testaments for $12.95, but this wasn't the case two thousand years ago.

The Gospel of Mark

The oldest book in the New Testament is the Gospel of Mark, which was supposedly written about forty years after the death of Jesus.[4] Again, though the book was given as "Mark," no one knows who wrote the book. In this book, we encounter Jesus at the age of thirty, and we are given no information about his life before this. For example, there is no account of a virgin birth in the Gospel of Mark. If you want to know more about his family life, personal life, teachers, and students, there is a great book called *Urantia*.[5] But the Gospel of Mark begins with Jesus as a thirty-year-old man who has students and tells stories and then dies on the cross. Yet, there is a tremendous amount of wisdom in this small book.

Jesus as an enigma

The first thing to know about the Gospel of Mark is that in it Jesus is a mystery.[6] Sometimes we encounter strange or exciting people in our lives, and we meet these people when they're in their thirties or forties or seventies. Something inside us tells us that something is interesting about this person, and we begin to ask all these questions: "Where are you from? Who's your dad? Who's your mom? How did you get this way?" We become curious, ask all these questions, and imagine all these possibilities, trying to figure out what is happening with this person. But in the Gospel of Mark, we have

---

4. Kingsbury, *Christology of Mark's Gospel*.
5. Urantia Foundation, *Urantia Book*.
6. Wrede, *Messianic Secret*.

no idea who Jesus is or how he has attained his wisdom. All we know is that this man enters into a town, looks at these people, and they begin to follow him. Jesus becomes a magnet, and the right people become like paper clips. The interior of some of those who are physically close to Jesus Christ, like Matthew or John or Mark, begins to change. They spiritually recognize that Jesus has something that they want, but what they want they don't know. All they know is that they are attracted to this man, but not physically.

Anthropologists, psychologists, and a few other specialists came together and looked at the geography and climate of the ancient Near East to imagine how people looked in Jesus's particular environment.[7] And they came up with an image that is not very flattering. Knowing this, we now have to sit back and ask, "How could anyone with common sense follow a man who is so physically unattractive?" This is important for the following reason. Though this new image of Jesus is an expression of physical unattractiveness, there was something profoundly, invisibly attractive about this man. He could walk into people's souls, wake those souls up, and give them an experience that they had never had before. There is a poem from Rumi, the Persian poet, where he says that it is true that the physical body has five senses, but our souls also have five senses.[8] If your soul has an eye, your soul can see the soul or spirit that lives inside this man called Jesus. Whatever the reasons were, despite his physical appearance and youth, he had the power to attract both young and old. In the Gospel of Mark, all he has to do is look at a human being, and if that person is at the right place in life, he says, "Follow me," and it's done.

Jesus is misunderstood

Jesus is known as a "rabbi," which means "teacher." In the Gospel of Mark, he doesn't consider himself God, nor do other people believe him to be God. His disciples are not portrayed kindly. Only Peter can recognize Jesus as the Messiah. Jesus tells his disciples and people what's wrong with them and he means that they lack understanding. He doesn't raise Lazarus from the dead. He doesn't say "I'm Logos," or "I'm God," or "Before Abraham, I was." In the Gospel of Mark, he tells lots of stories, but no one can understand those stories. In fact, in the Gospel of Mark, Jesus himself is constantly misunderstood.

7. Nickle, *Synoptic Gospels*.
8. Nicholson, *Mathnawi of Jalaluddin Rumi*.

If we think of Jesus Christ in the Gospel of Mark not only as a human being but as a symbol for wisdom, there are a couple of things worth mentioning about wisdom. We have no idea what wisdom is or where wisdom comes from. It has no parent, and wisdom has no friends. Wisdom is never understood, and wisdom is always alone. Wisdom can only express itself through stories. You can never see wisdom, and we never understand or recognize wisdom because wisdom is not linear or direct. For example, imagine what you do when you go out on a date. You go to a coffee shop and talk about your school and your work and your family and your past, and in the hour you spend at the coffee shop, you try to speak about who and what you are a thousand times straightforwardly, but still feel like something is left unexpressed.

There is another mysterious thing in the Gospel of Mark. All of us are lovers of wisdom. We seek wisdom because it beautifies our life. For those of you who like to go on dates or those of you who are looking for a lifelong companion, or those of you who want to read books, you are doing nothing but seeking perfection. But though people have no choice but to be attracted to wisdom, they can't understand it. They want to have it, and they love to be around it, but they can't have it. The closest people to this man of wisdom doubted him and ultimately betrayed him.

How does this help us? Everyone has had firsthand experiences about serious things in life. Maybe you watched your parents slowly die, maybe your boyfriend left you, perhaps you wanted an A in a class but you got an F, maybe you watched the Earth open up because of an earthquake and you just saw your entire life vanish, swallowed in a second. Whatever the cause, you have suffered a good amount of grief and loss. There is a good chunk of wisdom you gain from your experience. Whenever you have firsthand experience, it's not a plagiarized experience—it belongs to you. You are the owner of that wisdom. You have no choice but to share that with others, especially your friends. But if you are a good student of the Gospel of Mark, you will not expect your friends to understand. They won't. They will listen with the ears of their head, but what you are looking for is the ears of the heart and the soul, and that is not what your friends give to you. They will listen to your experience with the ears of their head, which are connected to the mind.

The mind is nothing but a machine that is socially manufactured with ideas, thoughts, a past, and culture. Because they lack experience, they will do much comparing and contrasting. These people live in Rome and are guided by Caesar, symbolically speaking. Just if you went out and wanted to tell people about what you went through, expect to be misunderstood, expect to be betrayed, expect the loneliness, expect the depression. That's the message from the Gospel of Mark.

The Stories of Jesus

In the Gospel of Mark, we find Jesus to be a tremendously good storyteller. Ask him any question, and he'll tell you a story. Direct answers will never work if you want to figure out who and what you are. Therapy will never work. Jesus recognized this some two thousand years ago. If you want socks, someone can give you directions to Ross, but if you're going to look for your soul, it's a puzzle that you have to discover because at first your soul is like a mustard seed—it's tiny and therefore needs time to grow and mature. You just have a feeling about it, but you can't see it or smell it or touch it. And Jesus says, "All you have to do is sit there, nourish it, and then wait and wait and wait, and maybe, if you are lucky, you will see it sprout. And if you can wait some more, maybe you'll see a trunk, and maybe you'll see branches. But you have to wait." But people sit there and say, "What is he talking about? Is he talking about the mustard seed?" This is a man who's come to realize that self-knowledge, self-understanding, and the human quest towards wisdom can only be expressed through story and metaphor. For example, if you love someone, you don't just say, "I love you." Instead, you give them chocolate and flowers because your actions become metaphors for love. There is no direct language regarding religion and spirituality or understanding oneself. *Everything* has to be metaphoric.

The problem that Jesus encounters in the Gospel of Mark is that he keeps getting misunderstood by his disciples, the very people who claim to be closest to him. No one understands him! Consider for a moment that you have a man who has spent an enormous amount of time trying to figure out what it means to be a human being, living with the most challenging questions a human being can ask, such as whether God exists and how to have a soul. In this book, Jesus understands all this stuff. Yet, do you realize how enormously lonely this man is? He wants to give us something, and language is the only tool he has. So he uses language to tell stories, only to realize that he is made even lonelier because no one understands the stories.

For us, of course, it is really easy to understand the New Testament and the wisdom of Jesus Christ because these books tell us that he was the Messiah. But two thousand years ago, when he was talking and walking, no one recognized this man. They said, "He's got some wisdom, and there is something rather unique about him," but still, he kept getting misunderstood.

For those who have had genuine experiences in life, you realize that direct communication will never work. You can't just tell someone how you're feeling, so you cloak your feelings within a story, and then you hope that this person understands. Then when they give their commentary, you realize that they are so far off. And then you say to yourself, "Why did I even open my mouth?" In the 1949 book *In Search of the Miraculous*, which is about the philosopher G. I. Gurdjieff, the first thing Gurdjieff asks of his students is, "You're going to come to my house, and I'm going to tell you many secrets. Share nothing with anyone."[9] And people would say, "But my wife, my husband, my best friend—surely they will understand." And Gurdjieff says, "Listen, you can share with them later, but for the next few months, just keep your mouth shut." And they say, "Okay." There comes the point in the book where Gurdjieff looks at these disciples and says, "Listen, if you want to go and talk to your best friend about the things that you've learned in this community, go tell them." These people go out, they tell their husbands, their wives, their friends, their parents, and their pastors, and they go back to Gurdjieff and, frustrated, say, "No one understands what we're talking about. They tell us that we've gone crazy! My best friend tells me I'm crazy!"

In the Gospel of Mark, Jesus symbolizes a human being with tremendous awareness. Jesus attempts to share this awareness through stories, only to be misunderstood. Why? Because people generally don't listen with the ears of their soul; though they may want to understand the stories, they can't. These stories are meant to be felt, not understood. For Jesus Christ, the mind is useless. You have to feel this stuff.

The garden of Gethsemane

Then there comes the point in the Gospel of Mark where Jesus is in the garden of Gethsemane, and for the first time we see a man who is kneeling, who is praying, and he says, "I don't want this anymore. Let this cup pass by me." Why would someone like Jesus find this path to be so burdensome

---

9. Ouspenski, *In Search of the Miraculous*.

that even though he is a man of God, he says, "I don't want to do this anymore. It's just a bit too much." You have someone so sure and with so much faith, and suddenly you see a broken man in this scene.[10] In the garden of Gethsemane, Jesus says, "I want to be ignorant. I don't want to know, and I do not want to carry this wisdom anymore." But a few minutes later, he catches himself and says, "Forget that. Thy will be done." Later on in this book, he finds himself on the cross, and on the cross we encounter a profoundly lonely man. He has lost God, he has lost friends, he is all alone on the cross, and he cries out, "My God, my God, why have thou forsaken me?" This is a man who no longer has a soul, a man who is all body. He wants someone to help him, but there is no one out there.

What this book suggests is the following. Every one of us has had troubling experiences that have broken us, and out of the brokenness we have wisdom and insights inside us. We try to communicate them to other people, only to realize that no one understands. Nietzsche, the German philosopher, used to say, "When people feel and understand, there are only two things that they can do. They can either cry or laugh. Mostly we cry."[11] Language and friendships fall apart, faith is broken, and nothing remains.

This is the fate for seekers of wisdom. Wisdom will make you alone. It will leave you without friends, unable to communicate or be understood. You will become an outcast, and the social forces will be so enormous that you will begin to doubt yourself, and you will have your garden of Gethsemane. You will recover, only to find yourself on the cross saying, "I did all of this, for whom? For what?" Because not even God will be there to support you. At least, that is how you will feel—abandoned. This is something that every parent endures. If you have a father or a mother who tells you, "Don't drink, don't smoke, stay in school," what do teenagers do? They will rebel. And ultimately, what will the parents say? "I can't do anything." They feel all alone, and their wisdom is rejected. Late at night, they lay in bed with their spouse and say, "How else should we communicate with our child? He doesn't understand." And the wife or husband says, "Ah, leave him alone. He'll learn, the hard way."

We have no idea how teachers are made. They are mysterious. We don't know where Jesus came from or how he got his wisdom. One of his disciples says, "You're a rabbi"; the other states, "You're the Son a God";

---

10. Brown, *Death of the Messiah*.
11. Nietzsche, *Basic Writings*.

another says, "You're just a teacher." Wisdom is always misunderstood; it always falls into doubt, ultimately crucified. That is the Gospel of Mark.

Why do people want to share their wisdom with other people?

Wisdom is like being pregnant. You can hold wisdom inside for some time, but eventually your child, wisdom, needs to come out. Wisdom is there to be shared with others. It's like the difference between eating food alone and eating food with your family and friends. Food has a different taste and quality when shared with others, and likewise there is something very social about wisdom. Wisdom desires to be seen, to be known, to be shared. But wisdom, symbolized by Jesus, never sees or cares for itself and never speaks of itself. It's always for another. However, when we get to the Gospel of Judas, we will see that Jesus realizes that, though people want wisdom, there are no good customers for wisdom, so he closes the wisdom shop and goes home as there are no buyers. We sometimes have this experience in our lives, but the difference between Jesus and us is that we walk away from a single person, whereas he walks away from all of us. His situation is more serious. We will never know how someone like Jesus is made. These people can give us some stories, but it is unknown how these stories transform themselves into a piece of wisdom. This is a mystery to which no one has access.

The Gospel of Matthew

The Gospel of Matthew was written about fifty or sixty years after the death of Jesus, which is important because each gospel gives a different set of events.[12] The Gospel of Matthew has stories and episodes that the Gospel of Mark doesn't have.[13] For example, Jesus is more social in the Gospel of Matthew, but, very much like in the Gospel of Mark, he comes to realize that people are unable to receive his wisdom. In the Gospel of Matthew again, he also finds himself on the cross, and he feels lonely.

In the Gospel of Matthew, unlike the Gospel of Mark, we are told that Jesus Christ is born of a virgin. Her name was Mary, and she was never touched by her husband, Joseph. It's essential for Christ not to be born of human flesh, as God was intimate with Mary, not Joseph. It is true that, on

---

12. Edwards, *Matthew's Story of Jesus*.
13. Brown, *Birth of the Messiah*.

the surface, Jesus looks like us, but there is a part of him that belongs to God and cannot be shared with anyone

The Gospel of Matthew is a Jewish gospel, as seen in the genealogy at the beginning of the book.[14] The genealogy is a family tree that takes Jesus back to Abraham. There is a reason why the genealogy goes back to Abraham, who is considered the father of the Jews. When a person possesses wisdom and specific life experiences, they want to share this wisdom and experiences with other people, but these things can only be shared with familiar and intimate people. In this book, Jesus loves his people, the Jewish people, and his wisdom is limited to the Jewish people.

The Gospel of Matthew was meant to do one thing for the reader's psychology. He is the fulfillment of the promise that was given in the Torah, the Old Testament,[15] that the Messiah would come from Egypt and fulfill the prophecies. And what Jesus does in the Gospel of Matthew is that he looks at his people, their needs, what sort of poverty they have, and he take the philosophy from Moses and he changes it into a language and philosophy that fit the needs of his people. When you look at the Gospel of Matthew, the message is less about finding "the kingdom of heaven within you" and more about social justice. If you see someone who has no clothes and the weather is freezing, the kingdom of God and going to the mountain and reflecting, meditating, and praying is not useful. You serve God by going to a store, buying a jacket, and giving it to a homeless person. If you find someone who is hungry, don't tell him, "Man doesn't live by bread alone." Go to Subway, buy him some food, and then give it to him.

The Beatitudes

Each tradition has its paths or methods. For example, the Hindus have four paths of yoga: *bhakti, raja, jnana,* and *dharma*; the Buddhists have the Four Noble Truths and the Eightfold Path; and the Taoists have the five characteristics of emptiness, formlessness, water, being like a child, and creativity. In the Gospel of Matthew, Jesus Christ gives us eight steps called the Beatitudes.[16]

All the eight steps start with "Blessed." The Beatitudes are all blessings that have to come down to us. We can't reach them through our efforts, no

---

14. Allison, *New Moses.*
15. Senior, *What Are They Saying about Matthew?*
16. Perkins, *Introduction to the Synoptic Gospels.*

matter what we do. Someone or something up there must like you. If you ask someone for ten dollars, but the person who has money doesn't like you, they're not going to give you any money. They're not going to bless you with ten dollars. We can't force someone to like us, and we especially can't force someone to love us, no matter how much or how hard we try. Blessing is like grace—it comes down. You can't be a stranger, come to a person, and say, "I need ten bucks," unless that person happens to have a tremendous amount of empathy, sympathy, and compassion within them, which takes a long, long time to cultivate and reach maturity. This is also not pity, where you look at someone, feel sorry for them, and then give them ten bucks. Someone needs to look at you, needs to see that your heart is broken, and then provide this thing called the "kingdom of God" to you. It's like money. But you have to be interesting enough to be looked at. You need to be attractive enough to be desired, and since Jesus is not a physical teacher but a spiritual teacher, he must like your soul. If he doesn't, he's not going to give you anything. He doesn't promise you physical pleasure, and he doesn't promise you a car or a house or a degree. He offers something that's not tangible.

We will only cover six of the eight Beatitudes, and all of these commandments could be condensed into the first Beatitude: "Blessed are those who are poor in spirit, for they shall inherit the Kingdom of God." But this poverty is a mystery. Just as no one knows how anyone could be gifted a blessing, no one knows how anyone could have a spirit that falls into poverty. The truth is, if you want money, you'll just go to your father and beg him to give you ten dollars. But you know where your father is, and you know what you want, and if you have a relatively good relationship with your father, he'll give you the money you ask for. But no one knows how to create a spirit that lives in poverty. No one even knows where to find an entity, namely God, who enjoys people with poverty of spirit. And no one knows how long someone poor in spirit needs to wait to be given the kingdom of God. No one even knows if the first Beatitude is humanly possible. How do we become attractive to God so that God can provide us with a soul and then plunge that soul into poverty so that soul can start begging and praying? This is a heart or a soul that wants to fall in love with his wife but can't, or that wants to fall in love with his children. There is nothing that this heart can attach itself to, and it remains broken, always a ditch, always ready for the water.

The second Beatitude is, "Blessed are those who are broken, or those who mourn." Sometimes we suffer grief because we are physically or socially isolated or lonely. It's mourning, but this particular grief goes back to our physical body. Sometimes we regret and grieve because we have no money, and this particular grieving goes back to the absence of power. Sometimes we argue with our companions and then grieve. That particular mourning goes back to our physical relationship with another human being. But Jesus Christ doesn't care about our friends, money situation, or marriage. He cares about our souls. But we have no idea how to have a soul that mourns for fulfillment. In the Beatitudes, Jesus shows us that he wants to give his students the soul that lives inside him. Once the teacher's soul lives inside the student, the student begins to pray and weep, until finally the student begins to find their soul that functions in its unique way.

The third is, "Blessed are those who are meek." Every person in poverty mourns. There is no grief without poverty of some kind, and poverty always signifies a loss. When there is poverty, there is brokenness. There is meekness, humility, insignificance, and irrelevance when there is brokenness.

The fourth Beatitude is, "Blessed are those who thirst and hunger." For those who want to know what thirst and hunger are, fast tomorrow. Don't eat or drink anything, and you'll realize that when food is kept away from the body, we lose interest in physical things. Your body doesn't have the energy to be interested in anything. All you do is sleep, and hunger prolonged becomes depression. All of a sudden, food becomes the most important thing in life. In the case of this Beatitude, one must thirst and hunger for truth. This means that one cannot find nourishment or contentment in anything because their only desire, the only Sabbath, is discovering the truth, embodying truth, and expressing truth.

The fifth Beatitude is, "Blessed are the merciful, or the compassionate." John Calvin, a companion of Martin Luther around the fifteenth century, said you should never harm another human being because in them lives the image of God.[17] So when you injure, hurt another human being, you're hurting God. In some ways, mercy is an act of forgiveness, and although someone has wronged you, you still show them kindness.

"Blessed are the pure-hearted" is the sixth Beatitude. Rumi, the Persian poet, once said, "Every teacher I find wants to write something on my consciousness. I am looking for a teacher who can erase what my parents, religion, society, and fantasies have written upon me. Because all these are obstacles to my spiritual growth."[18] This is what it means to be pure in heart.

17. Calvin, *Institutes of the Christian Religion*.
18. Nicholson, *Mathnawi of Jalaluddin Rumi*.

The Gospel of Luke

The Gospel of Luke was written about seventy years after the death of Jesus.[19] In the Gospel of Luke, the genealogy of Jesus is different. In the Gospel of Matthew, the genealogy of Jesus goes back to Abraham. In the Gospel of Luke, the genealogy is traced back to Adam. This is because in the Gospel of Luke Jesus says, "I will give my teaching to anyone willing to receive. I will go to an unknown location and find myself among strange people to give them what my people reject. Since my own people don't like me, I may find someone who doesn't look like me but will embrace my teaching and my wisdom." The Gospel of Luke tells us to pay attention to where people are, what they need, and what culture they come from. Most often, we will not be received by our own people. There is a saying in the Gospel of Luke: "A prophet is never welcome in his hometown." For example, if you are married, don't teach or instruct your companion because that's not why you entered the relationship.

What the Gospels of Mark, Matthew, and Luke have in common is the following.[20] Whenever people ask Jesus Christ a question, he always responds with a story. For example, people ask, "What is God?" He tells a story. "What is marriage?" He tells a story. While he is hanging on the cross in the Gospel of Luke, he does something that isn't found in the other gospels. He looks up above him and says, "Father, forgive them, for they know not what they do." He doesn't say this in the Gospel of Mark or the Gospel of Matthew. If we have a piece of wisdom that we want to give to others, we try to give it to our own people, but they won't understand. Then we try to give to anybody willing to listen, but they too won't understand. In the Gospel of Mark, he repeatedly says that people cannot understand. But in the Gospel of Luke, Jesus has learned that it's not that people don't want to understand the truth, or become wise, or beautify their life. The truth is that they don't have the capacity. It's not that people don't want to leave their undesirable neighborhood, buy a Tesla, or own a nice house. The truth is that they just don't have the financial resources. It's not their fault. The only thing you can do with people is forgive them, understand them, and exercise compassion, empathy, and sympathy.

---

19. Cadbury, *Making of Luke-Acts*.
20. Brown, *Birth of the Messiah*.

CHRISTIANITY

Fyodor Dostoyevsky and the three temptations

There is a book written by a Russian philosopher named Fyodor Dostoyevsky about one of the first scenes in the Gospel of Luke, called "The Three Temptations of Christ." Dostoyevsky shows us the complexities of this man named Jesus and the difficulties of following the path of Jesus.

Like most Russian philosophers, Dostoyevsky wrote massive books, and this one is entitled *The Brothers Karamazov*.[21] Chapter 5 of book 5: it's Easter, which, of course, is celebrating the resurrection of Jesus Christ. This episode occurs around the fifteenth century, during the Spanish Inquisition, when everybody is joyous and celebrating in anticipation of the second coming of Jesus. All of a sudden, people have this strange feeling. They say, "We don't understand why we feel this way. It seems that there is someone amongst us who is a *mahatma*, a 'great soul.'" And they look to their right and they look to their left, and all of a sudden a man appears, from apparently nowhere. He has long, black hair, a beard, and blue eyes, and they intuit that this is Jesus Christ. Suddenly, the Grand Inquisitor also sees that this is indeed Jesus Christ from his balcony. "But Jesus should not be walking freely amongst people," he thinks to himself. So the Grand Inquisitor comes down, grabs Jesus by the neck, and takes him by force to the dungeon, and says, "What are you doing here? Do you know it took us—Rome, the Vatican, the papacy—fifteen hundred years to give people a sort of Christianity that they enjoy? Don't you know that we have the power to create inside people's thoughts and emotions? We give them dreams, hopes, and imagination. You can't just come here, walk freely, talk to people, perform miracles, and destroy all that we have done." And then he goes on to say that the pope has more power than Jesus Christ, and Jesus is a foolish man because he didn't listen to Satan when Satan offered him three temptations.

In the Gospels of Luke and Matthew, Satan appears to Jesus and presents him with three temptations.[22] The first temptation that Satan offers Jesus is this: "You know that you're going to be misunderstood. You know that no one's going to follow you out of their own free will. Your path is far too frightening and difficult. Invite people to follow your path by turning every stone into bread. Then people will follow you for sure."

---

21. Dostoyevsky, *Brothers Karamazov*.
22. Maddox, *Purpose of Luke-Acts*.

We all have to have a job or chase the money because we need to pay rent, utilities, and gas. What does Satan offer Jesus Christ? "If you think that people desire happiness—not the happiness of the body but happiness of the soul—then free them from the physical bondage. Ensure that they don't ever have to work a job where they feel exploited. Because if people know that there is always going to be bread in the kitchen, that there will always be the money for rent, and that physical security is always there, then people can go to the church every day. People can read books and cultivate their intellect, emotions, and spirit. Physical life is far too distracting." And the Grand Inquisitor, who is like the pope, looks at Jesus and says, "You're a foolish man because Satan offered you this way out and you said, 'No, thank you.' You said, 'I want people, individual persons, to follow me because they love me and because they wholeheartedly want to follow me.'" Do you not see how difficult it is to be a physical human being? The temptations that live in life? The fears that we have? The insecurities? Do you know how difficult it is to make money and find a job that is an extension of our soul? Who wants to go to school? Who wants to work at In-N-Out? And yet, we have to. And then when we die, we meet God, who will judge us and then condemn us for not being able to worship him the right way. All this could have been corrected some two thousand years ago: Make sure every belly is full. Make sure that everyone has a roof over their head. And people will reflect, think, and be more spiritual rather than merely physical. But that is not what Jesus did, because he was selfish and shortsighted.

The second temptation is psychological: "Jump from this building, and then the angels will catch you before you fall. People will be dazzled, and then they will follow you because you're a magician." And Jesus says, "I don't want to exploit people emotionally. That's not my job." We watch movies because they are mysteries. We read books because they contain secrets. We go out on dates because a new person is a mystery. We travel because new places are mysterious to us. We are organisms that, without mystery, fall victim to boredom and despair. And all Satan is suggesting is, "Look. Physical life is mysterious, true enough. But make yourself so mysterious that people will follow you. And then when people follow you, where exactly are you going to go? You're going to go to church! And when people follow you, they will go to church as well, instead of the places that they usually want to go to waste time and, consequently, their life." And again Jesus says, "No. I want people to choose me freely."

Next is the political temptation. Satan asks Jesus to bow to him and kiss his feet. And Jesus says, "No. I'm not going to do that." Satan replies, "But if you do, I will make you the king of this world." How many of us want someone just and wise to occupy the White House? How many of us want a king who will give everybody healthcare? Free education? All of us. All that Jesus has to do is to kiss the feet of Satan. But he says, "No."

Dostoyevsky believed in human fragility. That we are far too weak and have a broken spirit. We are incapable of exercising humility, and we are far too arrogant to be able to hunger and thirst for righteousness. We can't make individual efforts because it's too much work, and we don't have the proper desires or the sufficient tools to cultivate our minds and souls. But maybe Jesus was right. He wanted people to follow him for the right reasons, not because they wanted physical benefit from him.

The Gospel of John

The Gospel of John was never meant to be a part of the New Testament, because it's so different.[23] In this gospel, not a single story or parable can be found, and it is the only gospel where Jesus says, "I am God," and, "I'm the bread; I'm the light. If you see me, then you see God." This book is also unique because it is filled with miracles, and it seems that Jesus realizes that talking doesn't work. When you communicate through language, you will always be misunderstood because you deal with people's biases, limitations, and shortcomings, which are all injected into language. Jesus bypasses all of that by doing something extraordinary—he performs miracles.[24] People will be dazzled if you turn water into wine or multiply fish. Though it is fantastic, we need to understand that when Jesus communicates through miracles, not language, he has lost hope in people's capacity to receive, understand, and process what he is giving them. He seems to lose hope that people are interested. Jesus realizes that this fantastic machine called the human brain is good, but people don't use it correctly. He no longer has any reason to talk anymore, and he has people follow him not because they understand but because he has inspired them through their feelings.

To put this another way, some of us have relatively insightful and wise parents. They know that when we grow up in Oakland, or other areas that are not so nice, especially when we have dicey friends, we will be exposed

23. Ashton, *Understanding the Fourth Gospel.*
24. Kysar, *John, the Maverick Gospel.*

to certain things. Parents know that sometimes their kids go out with these kinds of friends, so what do some parents do? Some parents will go ask their kids, "Why don't we go somewhere today around 6, and we will sit and talk and drink together?" Do you know what this does? The kids will begin to trust their parents and slowly have faith in their parents, and this faith and trust create psychological intimacy. Eventually, at least one hopes, these kids will have nothing to hide from their parents. They become open to different possibilities. Parents approach this problem in a controlled way to prevent their kids from falling into too much trouble. It's called magic. Parents will not sit and convince their kids that certain things are bad, because parents know human beings are not animals who receive advice well. By giving children firsthand experience, you appeal to their emotions and intellect.

Parents become magicians. If you are in a relationship where you want to go back and forth with your companion about why they think and feel a certain way, you will have to continue this conversation over and over until you die. People will never be convinced, and you will never be convinced by what they tell you. There is only one way to convince your companion: by being a magician. Performing actions for your companion or appealing to your companion's emotions is more effective than language.

Essentially, in the Gospel of John, we see a very mature teacher, and he doesn't tell stories but only performs miracles.

The Gospel of Judas

The Gospel of Judas, which was written approximately two centuries after the death of Jesus, was discovered in the 1970s.[25] In the Gospel of Judas, we find something interesting. In this gospel, Judas is the closest disciple to Jesus, and only Judas can understand the God part of Jesus, the soul of Jesus. Judas doesn't betray Jesus, and instead, Jesus asks Judas to free him from the physical world.

Jesus in the Gospel of Judas is not like the Jesus that we see in the other gospels. Jesus mocks the external forms of religious traditions, essentially saying, "They're all fantasies created by the human mind. These external things are false ideas with which we distract and entertain ourselves, and they're stories that we've made to make ourselves feel good." He doesn't take his disciples seriously. He's come to recognize how difficult it is to be

25. Bredar and Barrat, *Gospel of Judas*.

a good student and a good teacher, and he acknowledges that most people can't learn. Forget the common person—his closest disciples are no good.

He also comes to realize something unique about himself. As long as he lives in his body, he will fall victim to temptations. He'll always desire food, companionship, and power, but he wants his soul to be untarnished and uncontaminated. He wants complete freedom. In the Gospel of Judas, he says, "If you want your soul to be free, there is only one thing you can do. Find yourself a cross, and die. Physically die, because your soul is no longer held prisoner to your body once you are dead. It will go back home." For those of you who have been in love but the person you loved was far away, it seemed as if the world had shrunk. The world became so small that it began to suffocate you. And all of a sudden you got a message, "I'll be in town for two hours. I would love to see you if you have time," and something about you jumped out and rejoiced. What Jesus says in the Gospel of Judas is that the world is there to suffocate, destroy, and imprison us.

If we understand death metaphorically, death would mean getting rid of all the desires of physical pleasure, social status, and family life. Make sure that these three areas of life remain poor, so that you begin to intensify your longing for spiritual life. That is where your brokenness is. That is where your humility is. That is where your death is. And in your death, you will have access to the kingdom of God.

Christian Philosophy

Soren Kierkegaard

Soren Kierkegaard was a Danish Christian philosopher from the nineteenth century. An inwardly tortured philosopher, he has an interesting statement: "Melancholic people have the best humor."[26] Kierkegaard was an introvert and always lived with inner conflict, and because this tornado lived inside him, he could never really find peace. He was supposed to get married, but he couldn't because he loved God too much. But because of his love for God, he hated the world, so he hated God as well, and in the end he had nothing. He couldn't respect himself, so he didn't allow other people to respect him, so he hated *everything* about himself and life. But one of the things about people like him is that they're amusing. They're not funny because they are happy, but their sense of humor is a shadow of their tragic existence. You

---

26. Kierkegaard, *Either/Or*.

know how sometimes you go to funeral service after someone very close to you has passed, but the only way to cope is to laugh or look at your friends and tell jokes. Not because you are at a joyous occasion, but because humor is often the only way to cope with the tragedies of life.

Because of his great humor, Kierkegaard was often invited to parties, and he would be the sun, and on the center stage, and he would make everybody laugh. He would forget that he just walked out of his room, all alone, where it was dark, where he hated himself, where he hated people, where he hated everything, because at this party he would come to life. The only problem with things that come from our senses is that they are temporary. The last five minutes, ten minutes, maybe a day, perhaps a week, maybe two weeks, but eventually Kierkegaard knew that he had to walk home alone. And he would say, "When I leave a party—after being the sun, after giving warmth to everyone at the party—I walk home alone, and I am so depressed I want to commit suicide." This was a man who was indeed aware of the longevity of pleasure, the longevity of power, the longevity of being in a romantic or even communal relationship.

For the poor fellow Kierkegaard, he couldn't find a way out. He wrote a book called *Fear and Trembling* because he felt the presence of God on his insides, and many people consider him a passionate Christian.[27] But though Kierkegaard felt this presence within him, he remained the product of modern Western philosophy, so his approach to philosophy and life was profoundly intellectual, which means that many of his feelings and ideas lacked substance.

Georg Hegel

Hegel was a German romantic, idealistic Christian philosopher from the nineteenth century who believed that everything in life has a trinity.[28] For example, you walk into a room, but then the door behind you shuts and a door in front of you opens. You walk through this second door and find yourself in a different room, and the contents of this new room are very different, so you have to adjust yourself. Then you adjust yourself to the contents of the new room, and then you realize you need to go to another room. But you can only get to the third room by having gone through the first and the second rooms. Hegel argues that when things happen in life

---

27. Kierkegaard, *Fear and Trembling*.
28. Hegel, *Philosophy of Right*.

or when forces enter our lives, there is a struggle, and then there is this Sabbath, or this resting period, and then another force enters. It's like the Hindu idea of reincarnation, where things die, and new things come about out of the ashes of the dead.

Because of this, he argued that human beings can never know the reasons or truth behind specific experiences. If, for example, you're in a relationship and it's going badly, and you're weeping, and in despair and anger, you have no idea how you're going to view this relationship in two years. And if you properly approach Hegel, the truth is that none of us would dare to judge any experience because we have no idea how these experiences will shape us in six months or two years. Hegel argued that it's good to suspend all sorts of judgments because ultimately, as he said, "I can only get to know myself through my history. And my history will come to an end when I die." You submit yourself to the will of history. Life will do what it will with you, and you should not make too many judgments or have too many emotions about it. Eventually, there are nuggets of wisdom found in all experiences. Hegel's ideas of trinity, the different forces in life and history, are liberating philosophies of life.

Christianity and Platonism

Many of the words and ideas in Christianity are from Platonic philosophy, so one of the best ways to examine love in Christianity is to understand how love is portrayed in Platonic philosophy. One of the most important things that came to Christianity from Platonism is love, so to understand the different types of love in Christianity, it is good to examine how love was created between Socrates and Plato.

There was a woman about three thousand years ago named Diotima.[29] There is not much said about her, but she was the woman who created the man we know today as Socrates. We don't know too much about their relationship either, except that they had a very intense relationship for a very long time. She is known to have taught Socrates how to love, and she is the woman who gave Socrates his soul, his wings. Once Socrates became proficient in loving, he never went back to visit Diotima, and that's usually how good relationships between students and teachers are. Once you have served someone for ten or twenty years and done things the right way, staying with that person could become more poisonous than beneficial.

29. Plato, *Collected Dialogues*.

Socrates was a married man, and he had children. Ask yourself how his wife felt when Socrates would look at her every morning and say, "I am going to visit Diotima." And his wife was a young and attractive woman. Socrates wasn't a good father to his children, in that he wasn't there at all, and he didn't care to be. That's one of the things about people like Socrates, Malcolm X, and Mahatma Gandhi.

Something happens when you realize you have a soul. Your family, children, job, and self-image all belong to your body. And as long as you don't have a soul, or your soul happens to be very small, your family is very important to you, money is very important to you, and physical pleasures are very important to you. In the Gospel of Luke, Jesus says, "If you want to follow me, you need to know that you will grow to hate your husband, you will grow to hate your father, to hate your mother, to hate your sister, to hate your neighbor. I don't come to bring peace, but discord." Or, "Anyone who sits near me sits near fire." This is what happens when you have a soul. There is a conflict between your body and your soul, and though your soul wants God and inspiration, your body wants kids and stability. Socrates, by this time, has a soul that's ballooned, so every day he goes out, and he wants to make people pregnant, but not physically. He wants to grow a soul inside them. When someone has a soul, that person doesn't look at other human beings as bodies but as potential ovens where souls can be cooked. Socrates found himself commissioned by the gods to go out and breathe the spirit that lives inside him into other people. But even so, his wife was always angry with him. Even in the last days of his life, she went to the court, looked at the judge, and said, "He's been a bad father, and he's been a bad husband."

His wife would ask Socrates, "Can you go out and get some food for us?" He would go and come back five hours later, and his wife would say, "Listen, you went to go get milk because our son was screaming for food. It took you five hours, but it's was just five minutes away!" "Yeah, but on the way, I ran into someone, and I asked him what the meaning of his life was, and since he didn't know and had all these false assumptions about himself, I tried to educate him. That took like four hours. Then I ran into someone else, and he was married, and I asked him if he knew why he was married and if he knew what beauty was, and I realized that he didn't know any of this. And I realized that it's far better for me to educate these people. While engaged in these conversations, I completely forget about our kid's milk." His wife decided to hide his clothes so that he wouldn't leave the house. But Socrates was a social animal, not social in the sense of just having friendships, but in the sense that he wanted to inspire people and let them know they have a soul inside them that they had forgotten. And so his students, the people that loved him, who didn't understand him but loved him nevertheless, would take some extra clothes to him. And he would climb out of the window, and his students would give him the clothes, and he would go away and talk to people for five or six or nine hours, and then come back home.

Though he lived long before Jesus, Socrates had the faith described in Christianity. There is a saying from the Sermon on the Mount in the Gospel of Matthew, where Jesus says, "If you look at the birds, they don't think, they don't save, and yet they're fed." If somehow the soul about you comes to life, you'll find food. In Persian, there is a saying that allowing you to grow teeth will also provide bread. Socrates was that kind of guy. He just had faith. That if he's going to follow the calling of his soul, God was not going to abandon him. He lived until his seventies.

So we have a man named Socrates, and if you want to understand what was wrong with him, consider the following. If you want to know what happens when you have a lot of soul inside you, before you go to class or go to work, wake up at 6 or 7 in the morning and drink about ten gallons of water. And then go and sit, and something interesting will happen. For the first couple of hours, you're not going to feel anything. Then your body will say, "I need to go to the bathroom." If you just sit, your body will continue to say, "I need release; I need expression; I need freedom." So, very much like when you drink a lot and your body needs to get rid of it, when someone has a lot of soul, it kills them after a while if they don't release it. There is a saying in the Gospel of Thomas, "If there is passion inside you and this passion is not released, it will harm you."[30]

For example, imagine that you love someone, but they don't know that you love them. You have to keep this love inside you, and it can create a good amount of frustration, anxiety, even anger. And it doesn't matter if you're married or not. If you're in love with another human being and your wife or your husband looks at you and says, "Why are you angry all the time?" "Well, I just had a bad day at work." That's not true, and you know that! If you have a lot of passion inside you, if it's not expressed, it turns against you. So the next time someone asks you who Socrates was, say, "His soul had a lot of spirit inside it, and when he went out, he talked to people.

30. Ehrman, *Lost Scriptures*.

But when he talked, his words were like spirit, soul, and inspiration, and that is what philosophy is."

On one occasion, Socrates has a fortunate experience, which is that he runs into a tiny little man whose name is Plato. Plato is like any other young man in that he is filled with ambition and the desire for power. He's very tiny, and very insignificant, and though society may consider Plato to be a giant, in the eyes of Socrates, Plato is a man composed of meat. He has no soul inside him, but he has the capacity.

For whatever reason, though Socrates was quite proficient, fulfilled, perfect, and complete in many ways, he needed to express his spirit to someone, and that someone needed to receive that spirit in a way that pleased Socrates. It's like hands washing one another, and Socrates needed to find a soul that was ready to receive him.

Plato looks at Socrates, and he doesn't know why or how, but he feels that there is something profoundly attractive about Socrates. Just like Jesus, Socrates is a physically unattractive man. But because he has a soul, and because that soul is so grand, when Plato looks at him, it is not his face that he sees but his soul. When Plato looks at Socrates, Plato sees Socrates not with his physical eyes but with his spiritual eyes. But this is new to Plato. He doesn't know how he has grown the eyes of the heart or spirit. He knows what he's seeing: the sun, or the soul, inside the body of this man.

The first thing that happens is that Plato sees an image. Socrates is to him a billboard, and though Plato doesn't understand the image, something about this image entices Plato and brings something about him to life. Socrates also realizes that this little Plato can hold him. This is like a twenty-year-old going out with a fifty-year-old-man or woman, and the twenty-year-old body, mind, and set of emotions somehow can hold the experiences of a fifty- or sixty-year-old human being. Socrates realizes that Plato can embrace his gigantic soul, but Plato needs to be trained, which is where Plato's difficulties begin.

Plato is young, handsome, powerful, and rich, and he's got great parents who are politicians. He's all meat and no spirit. He wants lots of pleasure, but he also likes and enjoys the power and has a great family. His five senses are fully immersed in these worlds, but Socrates will introduce him to the world the senses can't reach. Socrates will take Plato to a place where Plato can't use his hands, legs, tongue. It's a world that he has to journey to, but not with his body, but with his soul, and it's going to be immensely uncomfortable.

Christianity

There is a tremendous amount of fear that overwhelms Plato. Because if he wants to follow Socrates, and if Socrates demands that he walk with the legs of his soul and the senses of the soul, it means all of Plato becomes irrelevant, and his history, identity, and privilege mean nothing. And for the first time, he experiences a kind of poverty that he's never experienced before. Socrates doesn't care for Plato's youth, money, power, or family. He cares for something we can't see and we can't touch. As many of us know, love is very easy to create, but its survival is difficult, and once it is established, ending it will be very difficult.

Although Socrates has created an image for Plato, imagine that suddenly an attractive woman walks past Plato. Now two images within Plato are competing, one physical and one spiritual. He can see, taste, touch, and smell one, and the other is a little abstract. If Socrates doesn't protect the image he's created inside Plato, Plato will shut his eyes to Socrates and open his eyes to physical beauty. It is very difficult to protect an image that someone has created inside you. Turn on the TV, pay attention to the advertisements, and you'll have AT&T, Sprint, T-Mobile, and Verizon within five minutes. They're all providing various images in hopes to intoxicate you, distract you, infect you.

This image created inside Plato has intrigued him so much that the intrigue turns into this thing called curiosity. As Plato progresses, he becomes a more active participant in understanding Socrates and himself. Intrigue and curiosity are emotional components. First you feel, and then you think, not the other way around. If you want a soul to be created inside you, the less knowledge or information you have, the fewer books you've read, the less reflective you are, and the more naïve you are, the better. Because this means that you have more capacity to feel. It should also be added that these ideas are usually better felt and understood by women. Women's reflection is about creativity, whereas men's reflection is about aggression and domination.

The images that Socrates gives Plato compete with 1,001 different images that assault Plato daily. Images or desires that come from pleasure, power, and family images. Do not underestimate this because if Plato leaves Socrates for a few months, the images of Socrates inside him will disappear completely. It takes a giant of a man to become a Plato. Not only must Socrates protect the image, but Plato must also have enough curiosity, interest, and passion for creating and pursuing this image.

Time is the only way to protect and nourish an image. When you spend a lot of time with someone, you create stories, a history, a relationship, a set of narratives, and intimacy. If you don't give time, all this will disappear. This time is designed to protect the image. Imagine if you read a book on philosophy, but then at 10:15 you read a book on geography, at which time your entire mental occupation revolves around geography, and after that around lunch, after that around math, and after that you go to work, and then when you go back home, someone asks, "So how was your day?" "The philosophy book was interesting, and the rest of them were interesting too," and then you collapse and go to bed. Philosophy will disappear very quickly. In the relationship between Socrates and Plato, there is an intense amount of devotion, passion, and worship. Plato doesn't need to go to a house of worship to find these things. One of the nice things about Plato is that he has found his Bible and his church in Socrates.

When curiosity is nourished, it turns into interest. Plato is now an active participant here, in that now he wants to understand. But the difficulty is that he can't. His mind may know where to get socks, but it does not know where to get the soul. Once time blossoms that interest, it turns into infatuation, which is dangerous and frightening. Here, Plato has emotions that he doesn't understand. There will be many contradictions, called *jihad al Akbar* in Arabic, which means a psychological battleground. Plato doesn't know why he likes Socrates. This is very strange because Socrates creates a lot of inner dialogue and conflict within Plato.

Socrates says, to paraphrase, "Family's no good, children are no good, money's no good; none of this stuff is any good. There is no reason for you to laugh or have a good time or go to parties. Nothing will make you satisfied, and nothing will make you happy." The problem with this is that we are creatures of habit. We like to conform and be validated by our society, culture, and environments. Whenever something unfamiliar enters your life, you will do whatever you possibly can to go back into a world that's comfortable because you want to laugh, and you want pleasure, money, and power. Plato sometimes walks back into this world, only to realize that now he has a good amount of Socrates inside him. Socrates ruins the party Plato wants to go to, casual conversation, and the plays that Plato enjoyed and wrote. Plato now wants depth, but his friends can't give it to him. They're far too incompetent and immature.

The problem with infatuation is that Plato is no longer in the power of anything. Plato wants to go home and focus on his life and writings, but he can't. Why? Socrates is there! Socrates has made Plato indifferent toward a whole host of things. All that has become important for Plato is Socrates. Socrates now lives inside Plato. And it's a dangerous place to be, especially for us in this culture. America is the land of individualism, autonomy, freedom, and advertisement. We don't like it when people tell us what to do and how to do it. We don't like to be ordered around. The English used to do that to us, and we ran away and created America. America is a place where we govern our own lives. When you become infatuated, you lose power and control, and another force goes inside you and begins to guide you, and you hate it for a couple of reasons. Biologically, we like stability and control. Infatuation is far away from anything domesticated and stable. The funny thing about infatuation is this. It lives inside you, and you think about ways to get rid of it, but the more you think about it and feel about it, it's like pouring lighter fluid on fire. It grows bigger, and suddenly you realize this is not infatuation; this is, in fact, obsession, and finally obsession turns into love. This is the relationship between Socrates and Plato, and this love is also the foundation of the love of Jesus expressed in the gospels.

Christianity and Modern Society

How is modern culture affecting religion and social relationships?

According to Hegel, society is evolving towards something.[31] We may lose a few billion people because of the particular evolution that we're going through, but eventually there is a brand new life and a new way of being human out of the ashes of life. Because most of us are used to human connections and relationships, it's difficult to see people on their cell phones all the time. But when, for example, two-year-olds are always screaming, "I want to watch cartoons," they get used to being alone and not needing any friends except a screen. Like Charles Darwin, the nineteenth-century biologist, would say, the human organism is wired to adapt to its environment, even to the loss of religion and social relationships.[32] So maybe the new generation will change the definition of marriages, relationships, and friendships. Perhaps they won't suffer the trauma we experience from these losses. We know what it means to have dinner with our parents, what it means to talk to our parents or friends on the phone. But maybe the new

---

31. Hegel, *Philosophy of Right*.
32. Darwin and Leonard, *On the Origin of Species*.

generation won't want the things that we desperately desire by the time they're twenty. Sixty percent of retail shops are closing because most people buy things online. In other words, people are okay with just sitting home, glued to their laptops, and ordering items. It is challenging to fill on-ground classrooms because most people want to sit home and do online coursework. We are becoming less and less social, and though it may be difficult for us, maybe the new generation won't have these difficulties.

It is also possible that if we were to be more attentive to human nature, needs, and desires, we would see that this won't be possible. That human beings are made to be social animals. And that we have particular biological and psychological needs and, unfortunately, technology won't be able to satisfy them all. We want friendship. We want to be caressed, we want to be looked at, and we want to be made visible by other human beings.

Is it possible to practice an inner form of religion in a secular culture?

Practicing an inner form of religion is too complicated in a secular culture. If you can go to school and get some book knowledge, then go to class and maybe even teach it, that's all you need. The rest is irrelevant. Western society has been so affected by modern culture and has become so secular that philosophy or spirituality is not necessary.[33] The best thing Westerners can do is make sure that we are emotionally and intellectually healthy. Westerners need basics for now. Find the right companion, which is challenging, get an okay job that pays the bills, buy a nice place that you can call home, have children, and raise them well. Since there is no community, we might create our own community. At this stage, the inner form of religion doesn't make sense unless there is a really good foundation. The first important foundation is parental, which creates a stable and meaningful community for their kids. Once this foundation is in place, then other things can be pursued. But if there are deficiencies in this area, it's best to do the basic stuff. There's nothing wrong with attending to obtain the essential nourishments of life: healthy relationships, steady income, and a nice place to live in. The basics are good.

We don't have to be philosophers. We don't have to be spiritual. We can just be regular people, which is more difficult than anything else. It's much easier to have a relationship with God than to have a relationship with a man

---

33. Talal, *Formations of the Secular.*

or a woman. With God, it's a one-way street: you give, and he usually rejects, saying, "You didn't do this right. Go back and redo this." A relationship with a man or a woman is very different since it needs to be two-way. You can feel the consequences of wrong thinking and wrong behavior and speech; in fact, you need to be much more mindful in a physical relationship than a spiritual one. In a spiritual one, you're obsessed with yourself, but in a human-to-human relationship, you need to come out of yourself and be there for another human being. And that's very difficult, especially in contemporary times, making us so selfish, self-centered, and egotistical.

There is no reason to read *The Interior Castle* by St. Teresa of Avila or *In Search of the Miraculous* by P. D. Ouspensky. These books are poison for the Western psyche, or any psyche at this point. Because the truth is, in many places in the Middle East, one out of every two marriages falls apart. It has the most opium users in the world. For example, 67 percent of Iran, a country in the Middle East, is under thirty-five. There are no jobs, no educational opportunities, and people do many drugs because there is little hope inside people. Rumi and Islam are not going to help them because it's the social condition of the country that creates these symptoms. You can sit in a cave and read all the Rumi that you want, but the truth is, no one's going to give you their daughter if you don't have any education or money. This means that you're always going to feel lonely, because from time to time your body demands that you sit next to someone and be comfortable, and you need to know that this person is going to be around for a long time. Maybe it's okay to be nomadic when you're young, moving from one person to another, but it will not be easy on your body, mind, and emotions as you age. It wears you out, and you become bitter and won't date or talk to anyone. While you are young and have all this energy, investing in the right things is not a bad idea. Middle age used to be fifty, but now we become old at twenty because we have so many complicated experiences that we are too young to understand and digest. So they make you inwardly worn out and old.

How can basic or secular life be lived religiously?

When you look at a bicycle wheel, the center and all the spokes go to it. That is what a religious society looked like before secularism dominated every aspect of life. Everything, from marriage, to raising children, to working to make money, revolved around religion. But there is no longer a center or a hub in people's lives or even society. Applying philosophical and religious tools is not easy without creating a center in your life. It takes too much effort, and finding a magnifying glass that can bring all the different forces of life to a single point and make it meaningful is very difficult. We are far too damaged by modern culture, and we are far too fragmented to make anything work healthily. Before the 1970s, if you had a car, that would be your car for the rest of your life. Your house and your job would last the rest of your life. Now, every two or three years, things change. A new house, a new job, a new relationship. The degree to which modern societies have given birth to human discontentment and dissatisfaction is enormous.

There is a tremendous amount of discontent in every person these days. And the question is, "How do you make this meaningful?" Perhaps it is not possible. Elizabeth Kubler-Ross argued that when there is something wrong with our body, we first struggle and fight to fix it, but then after a while we accept that the damage is not fixable.[34] It's like having cancer, and after like seven or eight months you accept the fact that you're going to die, and it may be a painful death. But at least you have made peace with the fact that cancer will overrun every part of your body, and eventually you will die, never seeing your hopes or dreams realized. But acceptance comes after a tremendous amount of pain. Unfortunately, there are many distractions for most of us, so we don't allow pain to penetrate. We jump from one relationship to another, whether it is a relationship with another human being or with video games, cars, jobs, or friendships. There are just too many distractions out there, which makes the right kinds of pain and the right kinds of acceptance difficult.

Forgiveness

What does it mean to be a sinner?

Because we don't have the complete picture of life or ourselves, we are born to be fallible and make mistakes. We don't have all the missing pieces of this grand puzzle called life. And because there are these missing pieces, there is a lot in our lives that remains in darkness, confusion, and chaos. No one has to condemn us. God, Satan, or even our parents do not need to condemn us. We could have the best of parents, but simply because much of life remains unknown for most of us, our future, our emotions, and our

---

34. Kubler-Ross, *On Grief and Grieving*.

identity will ultimately make us sinners because change is inevitable and difficult choices need to be made. We have no choice but to waste a lot of time and make a lot of mistakes, which will lead to regret, remorse, and guilt. Life speeds by very quickly. Just the awareness of that is exciting and inspirational. But it also makes us angry, especially when we talk to people who assume they know it all and have it all together. Ask people about relationships, and they say, "Oh yes, I know what a good marriage is." You talk to people who have degrees, and they say, "Oh yes, I'm a genius." You talk to young parents, and they say, "Oh yes, I'm a great mother or father."

Where *are* people going? Nowhere. Our lives revolve around assumptions because without them, we're nothing. For the most part, they're all fallacious and wrong, but what else can we do?

Now imagine that we bring God into this picture. God demands nobility, excellence, and perfection. That in itself is a tremendous condemnation because these demands force us into sin simply because we are far too incompetent to walk the path of nobility and excellence. We have no clue what they are, yet God and our own psychology push us to be perfect.

Jesus Christ argued that you have to believe in a different, invisible world and behave in *this* world in a completely different way. What about social and political pressures? What about capitalism? Capitalism creates endless appetites, makes us pursue unlimited desires, and gives us hunger and appetites that can never be satisfied. Even our very thirst for beauty will make us sinners. Imagine you go out with a man or a woman and say, "I love you." But your relationship lives in time, and time tends to decay things. Eventually, you will look at the same person and say, "When it comes to you, I've become a nihilist. I feel nothing about you. You have become completely meaningless. I used to have all these fantasies about you and our future together, but now when I look at my future, I don't see you in the picture at all."

It doesn't matter what branch you walk into in life; every branch offers its own unique and profound condemnations and definitions of what it means to be a sinner.

What is forgiveness?

Do you think you've ever said anything or acted in a way that offended someone else? Did you ever go home with a guilty conscience, thinking, "Maybe I shouldn't have"? Let's say that you've done something to someone, and you go to that person and say, "I'm sorry." And they say, "It's okay. Forget it. Let's move on." And even though this person has forgiven you, you still go home feeling bad, saying, "What is wrong with me?" Even though they've said, "You're forgiven," you have difficulty forgiving yourself.

Now, imagine that you come to understand why you did a thing, but the other person doesn't. They have categorized your action as bad or wrong. This person says to you, "You're an awful person, and I will never forgive you." Your understanding allows for forgiveness. That is, you forgive yourself because you understand why you did what you did. After a couple of tries, coming to realize that they're not going to forgive you, you say, "You know, I don't care." Being able to forgive yourself makes you indifferent to how that person feels about you.

Before we can talk about forgiveness, we have to ask, "What makes an action wrong? What makes an expression wrong? Any expression? Why would anyone deliberately, willingly do anything wrong?" A person has to be a psychopath to desire to hurt you. If this person is a psychopath, then forget it. They're exempt from this scenario. But if, on the other hand, this person is relatively sane and rational, the first question you need to ask is, "Why would this person do anything that would be hurtful?"

No one does anything wrong knowingly.

For example, sometimes people don't go to their classes or jobs. Their teachers and bosses are inwardly generous and exercise forgiveness and say to themselves, "Maybe the classes are boring and irrelevant. Maybe they've got other responsibilities. Maybe they're just not ready to grow up." Because if students knew the sort of information that is sometimes given in classrooms or the importance of having and keeping a job, maybe they would treat them differently. But for whatever reason, perhaps it's just their intellectual and emotional stage in life that does not allow them to take their work or school seriously. Do they want to get an F? Do they know that they're not getting any younger, but older? Eventually, graduating from college and having a resume will be very important in finding a well-paying job. They don't know any of that stuff. They are far too young and lack the proper experience. If they did, they would go to work and class regularly. But most young people don't do any of that stuff because they're not aware of the future or the importance of graduating or being employed.

For example, human relationships are very complicated, especially romantic ones. What usually happens is that we get into a relationship. You want something serious, but the other person wants something passing.

There is no denying that this other person is attracted to you, but they don't know why they're attracted, and they also don't know whether they want to stay with you long-term or short-term. But they get involved with you nevertheless. They don't understand their emotions or the anatomy of desires, but they get involved with you. Time passes, and they realize they don't want to be with you anymore. You're going to hold them hostage and threaten them with all sorts of nonsense because of some moral code and social norms that you don't understand.

To put it another way, you're held hostage by your expectations, and you want to impose these same expectations onto this other person, and you're going to try to make them feel bad by saying, "You're acting so immoral," and so forth. The truth is, you're both just occupying different stages in life. The truth is, we just don't know, and we have so very little understanding about virtually all aspects of life that we make mistakes all over the place. We have an awful GPS to life.

Consider Schopenhauer, the nineteenth-century German philosopher, argues that we have a blind "will" inside us.[35] We have no idea what it's doing. All we know is that it's just like a volcano, in that you're sitting, and all of a sudden it says, "Stand up! Walk!" "Where am I going?" The will doesn't care. It just tells you to do things, and some of the things that you do accidentally hurt people. You didn't know. It just happened. Imagine that Christianity is correct, and we're all stuck in *sin*, which is Latin for "missing the mark."[36] What do you expect from people living this life for the first time? We are bound to make mistakes. It takes a tremendous amount of insight, knowledge, experience, intuition, and wisdom to look at *all* people and say, "Oh! Another novice. Another infant is about to make a mistake. It'll be okay."

When you ask about forgiveness, the truth is, there is a concept of right and wrong, and we say that someone has overstepped certain boundaries and now they have to be punished or forgiven. But if you look closer, there is nothing to forgive. No one does anything wrong, and none of us know what we're doing, and that's just the way things are.

---

35. Schopenhauer, *World as Will and Representation*.
36. Nicol, *Mark*.

When does forgiveness become easier?

There is a saying from the ancient Chinese philosopher Confucius: "You can't make the grass grow by pulling on it."[37] Imagine you are thirty years old, speaking to a six-year-old child screaming for ice cream. You want to sit the child down, reason with them, and convince them that screaming for ice cream is not good. But the truth is, you're thirty, and you want to pull this child into being thirty, but they can't be pulled into that world because they're six. In society, we have the following.

There is a five-year-old who has a sibling that's two. There is a five-year-old who has a bigger brother who's ten. There is a ten-year-old who has a friend who's twenty. There is a twenty-year-old who has a parent who's fifty. A fifty-year-old has a father who's ninety, and the ninety-year-old has a friend who's on his deathbed. All of these people have different insights into life. A ten-year-old looks at the two-year-old sibling and says, "What an uneducated child." A two-year-old looks at a six-month-old and says the same thing. One of the reasons that there is no justice in society is because we all occupy different positions in life, and those positions give us different perspectives. The only thing you can do is sit back, watch people slip, then help them up and say, "You will learn in time. Hopefully, you will not make too much of a mess of your life." Because if they do, according to some religious perspectives, you have to come back and do this whole business over again. It is a mess. You just have to enjoy it, and the only way you can enjoy it is to have power over it, and the only way you can have power over it is to understand it well. And it's painful to understand anything well.

There is a poem from Hafez, a Persian poet from the fourteenth century. If I were to paraphrase it crudely, the point would be the following.[38] All of us are looking for a Joseph, but for some strange reason, some criminal has taken the most innocent, joyous, and happy and mature part of us, metaphorically called Joseph, and thrown it into a dark well. This Joseph keeps crying to come out, but we don't know how to bring him out. All of us are metaphorically like a Jacob. We shed tears because we want our son, innocence, happiness, and joy back. And Hafez says that eventually, despite the cruelties of the gods and the indifference of this world, your innocence and integrity will be given back to you. Maybe not today, perhaps not tomorrow; maybe, like in the book of Job, you will have to wait until you lose

---

37. Confucius, *Analects*.
38. Hafiz, *Faces of Love*.

everything in your life. But it will be given back to you. From the moment we're born, the human heart is home to sorrow, suffering, and betrayal. But Hafez says, "Don't worry. It's okay because there will come a time where this house of sorrow will be a place where beautiful flowers will grow."

The point of this poem is the following. Nothing in life is permanent. Be sad, but enjoy the sadness, because it won't last very long. Make sure that if sorrow comes to you, you write a poem or be creative in some way. If you're really sad, buy some food and give it to someone. All of us have lives and desires that we don't understand. Bad things happen to us, and we don't understand why. But it's okay because there will come a time where your curiosity and wonder will return, and all the conflict inside you and the veil of ignorance will be removed, and you will be given a glimpse of who you are. And when that glimpse comes to you, you will understand, and when that understanding comes to you, you will have your Joseph back.

What is the relationship between forgiveness and compassion?

A poem from the Persian poet Rumi says that when you imagine a rose that hasn't yet blossomed, and you can't even see the bud, all that can be seen is thorns.[39] But look at what is happening, Rumi argues. There is so much compassion inside the stem that it keeps forgetting and forgiving all these thorns. And out of that compassion emerges a bud, and then the bud opens, you see petals, and then you see the rose in its full glory. Compassion gave birth to this rose.

Imagine that someone comes to you and weeps and has so much sorrow inside them. If you exercise compassion in the right ways, listen to them and give them some attention, in time, the sorrow will turn into joy. In the movie *Mona Lisa Smile*, there is a scene where a young girl, Betty, is newly married.[40] Betty goes to another girl, Giselle, and says some nasty things. Giselle, who happens to be a little bit older and more experienced, allows Betty to say all these ugly things to her. And then, later in the movie, some things happen, and Giselle goes to Betty and holds her tight, embracing her with a tremendous amount of kindness and compassion, and this new bride breaks down and says, "He doesn't love me. He doesn't love me." Anyone else, after being told all these profanities, would walk away. Not this girl. Compassion removes anger and blossoms kindness.

39. Nicholson, *Mathnawi of Jalaluddin Rumi*.
40. Newell, *Mona Lisa Smile*.

Compassion is one of the most challenging emotions to express and one of the most difficult emotions to have in your arsenal, because we are born and wired to be self-centered. Imagine you are in a classroom or at work, and you see some cookies and juice on the table. And you are hungry and thirsty. Do you consider that other people might be thirsty or want some juice? Most of us don't consider any of that stuff. According to our own biological and psychological needs, most of us will take this food put it in our bag. Humans are wired to be profoundly selfish.

Because of this, compassion is very costly. To use the same example, you might look at other people and see that they're thirsty. There are a couple of things that can be done when you see others in pain. One option is that you can recommend that they go out and buy some water if they're thirsty, even though you know that you have extra juice in your bag. Or you could remember what pain is. Pain goes against our biology. We are not animals that embrace or live with pain well. The other thing you can do is override your own biology and put yourself in another's shoes. This is a person who could have no money in their pocket, nothing to eat, who sits in a room in a dignified, respectful way and says, "I'm thirsty." How would you feel if you were this person? Do you know the amount of imaginative creativity that's required to have compassion for another person?

But is it also an act of compassion when you allow someone to walk into your life and disrupt everything? In the Middle East, there is a saying: "If you want to know the limits of compassion, be kissed by a bee." For example, imagine you are sitting somewhere, and a bee comes and sits on your hand, but you tell yourself that brushing the bee away would be cruel. The bee has rights, you tell yourself, so you engage in an act of compassion and allow the bee to sit there. Suddenly, you scream, "Ow!" and within a few minutes your hand blisters due to the bee sting.

Nietzsche, the nineteenth-century German philosopher, argued that most of us exercise compassion in all the wrong ways.[41] Instead of helping people, he said, our compassion hurts them. True compassion is more than simply being kind to others. For example, when you are walking down the street or taking public transportation in the Bay Area, some women have their kids next to them, all under the age of five. The womon and kids are asking for money. Is it an act of compassion to take out a $20 bill and give it to her? Or is it an act of compassion to tell her she's exploiting her children, and they're going to have an awful future because of her? Is the real act of

---

41. Nietzsche, *On the Genealogy of Morality*.

compassion to make her feel bad about what she's doing to herself and to these kids, to realize that these kids will ultimately have no self-respect? Nietzsche argued that summoning strength and being harsh with people would be the greatest act of compassion for all right reasons. This is called education.

Imagine you were to go to your instructor's office, take off your shoes, and stretch out your legs. Your instructor is not your friend, regardless of how nice and kind they may act toward you. Seeing your actions, your instructor would punish you for the way you are behaving in the office by being so casual. It's their office, and they are three times your age.

Sometimes compassion has to do with specific goals in life. Your body may be starving and want food, but you also know that your spirit wants to soar. Out of compassion for your spirit, you punish your body. Sometimes you realize your spirit wants to soar, but your belly screams too much. From the compassion of your soul, you nourish your body. Fasting is the ultimate act of compassion one gives to oneself. For example, you say, "I no longer want to smoke, because it's bad for my lungs. I no longer want to drink, because it's bad for my kidneys. I no longer want to have casual intimacy, because it's bad for my body and emotions. I no longer want to scream, because I look bad in front of my kids." This compassion is problematic because it takes tremendous awareness and mindfulness. If you have a sister or a brother who is disabled or parents who are in pain, perhaps the best thing is to sacrifice your time, money, and energy and be with them. It's the best thing you can do.

It is an amazing task to take the sorrow of another human being and put it in your own soul. Consider these lines from the Gospel of Mark: "If you want to follow me, you have to carry the sins of the world on your shoulder. If you want to follow me, you have to find across and then follow me." If you want to be a Christian, your task is: do not judge. What does that mean? Everybody does things for a reason, and those reasons, for them, are legitimate.

3

Islam

The Life of Mohammed

ABOUT SIX HUNDRED YEARS after the passing of Jesus, there was a man in Saudi Arabia by the name of Mohammed.[1] One of the strange things about religious heroes is that all of them, without exception, have a mysterious birth and childhood. For example, Jesus, Mahavira, and Zarathustra are born of a virgin. Moses is put on a basket and picked up by strange folks, and Gilgamesh is two-thirds god, one-third human. Likewise, Mohammed has no father, and after a few years has no mother, so he is orphaned at a very young age. When he is four, angels come down, cut open his chest, and look into his heart. There are contaminations, so they cut open his chest, wash his heart, and put it back into his chest.

This takes place in the Middle East, in the middle of the desert, where food, water, and shelter are scarce, and protection of any kind is difficult. People's names and reputations mean everything. And if you lose your name, you lose your value in society, and without a tribe or social relations, you cannot survive. Everything about life is about physical power, because the more power you have, the more food you have and the stronger your support group. But this strange man named Mohammed does something interesting. Though he has a job and works, he doesn't know much about physical shelter, food, or money. From a young age, he begins talking to people about difficult, existential questions, such as, "I'm hungry, but not for physical food, but spiritual food, but I don't know where to go to be

1. Lings, *Muhammad*.

nourished. I talk to Jews, Christians, and my own tribe, the Bedouins, but nothing anyone says satisfies me." By the time he's twenty, he has become incredibly disappointed in people and their philosophies. So, he climbs a mountain and begins to make his home in the caves. He finds seclusion in this darkness, and sits and talks to no one. This man feels uneasy and asks troubling questions when people are more interested in physical power. This can also be taken as a symbolic story for people who once in a while ask spiritual questions but only find the darkness of their own psyche as their only companion.

The tragedy and the misery of this are profound and important. Imagine someone who has food but is unhappy. He has neighbors and companions but is discontent that he has money but is still dissatisfied. He looks at something attractive and is no longer moved. He has money in his bank account but is not excited. He has a house but does not feel at home and no longer cares for it. This is a human for whom the five senses no longer provide meaning and navigation for life. What is his fate? What should he do? There is something within Mohammed that seeks a home, but he doesn't know where home is and why he feels so uneasy about everything.

In this story, you have a young man who realizes he is doomed from a very young age, so he sits for hours in these caves, is quiet, and doesn't talk to anyone. This is how greatness is created. All these religious heroes have one thing in common: they have a yearning that takes place within them. And, like a clam, everything else about their life simply shuts down. Tremendous forces are generated within, and then this pearl, or wisdom, emerges after many decades.

Around the age of forty, something interesting happens to Mohammed. He hears a voice, which in the Islamic tradition is the voice of Gabriel, that says to him, "You need to read." But Mohammed says, "I am illiterate. I don't know how to read or write."[2] Paraphrasing, Gabriel replies, "The only thing that is worth reading is the writing on your heart, not your mind. And the only person that can write well on your heart or soul is Allah. You have been chosen by this thing called Allah."

The Arabs were naturalists, not monotheists, believing not in one God but many gods. In Arabic, *allah* means "idol" or "image." No one can go on a spiritual journey without having an image. An image is important as it subtly forces you into love. For example, we need to fall in love with another human being and feel the ups and downs of love. Then when there is

2. Jones, *Early Arabic Poetry*.

enough maturity inside you, you will remember your love experience and conclude that love has always lived inside you but needed a force, a push from the outside, to activate it. But the person with whom you had fallen in love becomes an image, a rope, a ladder. This image will make you illiterate to the writings of people but literate to the writings of God on your heart. People write on your mind, but God writes on your soul, and this is the only book worth reading.

Metaphorically understood, this is a stage in life that was, for example, also reached by a man named Aldous Huxley. Huxley was a twentieth-century philosopher who had read many books but came to realize that though he had read a lot, he truly hadn't experienced and understoodnd the things that he had read and written.[3] When we read and write, we want the words to come alive inside us, but if things are lacking, then the language cannot be brought to life, and after a while the words we write no longer go inside us. What is it that you want to read? What book has the wisdom to transform the very interior of your life? Becoming illiterate is a symbolic component of the spiritual journey, as there is nothing to read or write, and there is nothing to see and talk about. This is an enormous place of poverty, as expressed in the concept of emptiness in Taoism and the Sabbath in Judaism. Here is a man who has nothing to do, nothing to listen to, nothing to talk about, and he sits until the words of God come to visit him.

There is something very strange about Mohammed, in that he doesn't think that he is very special. After hearing this voice, he goes to his wife, who is about fifteen years older than he is, and says, "I've had this experience. I think I've gone crazy because no one has these experiences. It doesn't make any sense. Do you think my own mind is deceiving me?" His wife, Khadijah, says, "I can't answer that question, but I know a Christian monk who might help answering these questions." Mohammed goes to the Christian monk, and the moment the monk sees Mohammed, he says, "I see these signs around you, which must mean that the God of Abraham, the God of Moses, and the God of Jesus has spoken to you. It seems that you are on the same lineage and that you have become a prophet."[4]

This particular experience, the first time that God talks to Mohammed, is called, in Arabic, *leylat al qadr*, or "night of power." This is the birth of the sacred text of Islam, called the Quran. Just as the early Christians always sang the gospels, the Quran can never be read, but it must be sung.

3. Huxley, *Doors of Perception*.
4. Lings, *Muhammad*.

Though the book is a fantastic source of inspiration, we will never understand it. It was only for Mohammed, not the rest of us. The Quran is God's direct revelation to Mohammed and Mohammed alone, and the rest of us can only interpret and comment upon the book. All that we can do is impose our own bias-laden assumptions.

It took about twenty-two years for the Quran to come together, and because of the way the verses and revelations came about, there are many contradictions in the Quran because they apply to specific episodes or events.[5] A group of people called "People of the Rock" argued that each prophet has both the lion and the lamb within them. This means that the same message that applies to your physical life, which should you change your perspective a little, will also apply to your spiritual life. Likewise, the Quran has the literal aspect to it is as well as the metaphorical and esoteric or mystical aspect.

It takes two years for the next revelation to come to Mohammed. While he is waiting, he thinks himself to have gone completely mad. He wanted God to visit him, but God doesn't. Two years later, another experience, or revelation, comes to him or happens to him. Again, a revelation is written on his heart instead of his intellect. This experience, called *Naqshbandi*, becomes significant in the Islamic tradition. A couple of centuries after the death of Mohammed, there comes this group of people who argue that no one can teach us anything except God. God himself is the only person who has the right tools or pens to write on the human heart. Books can only write on your intellect, and though they can give you inspiring emotions, eventually they will fail because emotions inspired by books will not last very long. The *Naqshbandis* argue that the only thing that will have a lasting impact on us is when God comes down, finds our heart completely uncontaminated, and begins writing with his own pen. Once there is God's ink on your heart, your interior is forever changed, and, like a tattoo on your skin, you can never get rid of it. Instead of having someone write on your intellect, body, or emotions, the entire Islamic tradition is about having God write on your heart.[6]

The message of Mohammed is very much like the message of Moses in that it is rooted in social justice. Blacks need to be treated the same way as whites, and keep in mind that the first person to call people to prayer, whose name was Bilal, was black. Everybody needs to have a job, needs to

---

5. Arberry, *Koran Interpreted*.
6. Shah, *Sufis*.

have shelter, and no one should go to bed hungry. Mohammed undertook almost forty battles in the twenty-two years of his prophecy to ensure justice, peace, and equality in society.

Through Mohammed, the tradition called *Islam* comes about, which means "surrender" or "to submit." Islam is about accepting life, oneself, and society by living intuitively through having the voice of God come to life within and govern you. Submission means that this is the only voice that you will ever hear and the only voice that you will ever pay attention to and act upon. No other entity on this planet, especially any voice from society, is worth conforming to. Only the voice of God needs to be paid attention to. That is surrender and submission. You don't submit to the ways of society or your parents or your own desires. Instead, you only submit to the kingdom of God within you, which is foreign to the human mind, senses, and rationality.

What Does It Mean to Be Human in Islam?

Ensun

There are three ways of looking at the human being. The first sort of human is called *ensun*, which comes from the word *nos'y*, which means "forgetful," a concept that is also seen in other religious traditions.

In the Epic of Gilgamesh, Gilgamesh is forgetful because he is two-thirds god and one-third human, and he allows the one-third to take over for his entire life, and he forgets that he has God inside of him.[7] In Hinduism, the *atman* lives inside us, this pure self or sun that lives within. Most of us will get glimpses of this pure self, but fear overcomes us, and we turn away because it is so enormous and exciting.[8] We fall back into *Maya*, or self-deception, which we create for ourselves, usually for all the right reasons. In Buddhism, we forget that we have the Buddha seed inside us. We may realize that all things get old and diseased, but we ultimately become indifferent toward them. But we have no choice but to further distract ourselves with this and that, even though we know, deep down, that these pursuits will conclude in the same old place of emptiness and meaninglessness. We sabotage our own awareness and become forgetful. We all know that we have these moments where we actually "flow" in life. We know exactly

7. Sandars, *Epic of Gilgamesh*.
8. Smith, *World's Religions*.

what needs to happen, whether we should hold someone's hand, whether we should walk out of a job or a marriage, and in these moments these natural things tell us what we should do in life. But we bury them under an avalanche of forgetfulness or distractions because acting on them can be so traumatic. Confucianism recommends that we look at our parents' wisdom and struggles instead of acting upon our own whims and wishes. But often, in the name of freedom and exploration, we forget about the very tradition that gives us the navigational tools and guides and protects us in life. In Judaism, we are born and created in the image of God. But it is not easy to accept that we are walking gods, and after a while the physical life takes over. In Christianity, we forget that the kingdom of God lives inside of us, and we become Caesar. There are moments where we sit and watch a good movie and begin to cry or laugh, and, without knowing why, something magical oozes out of us. We want to protect these moments, but soon they fall victim to the distractions and demands of physical life.

In the Islamic tradition, this forgetfulness is called *ensun*. We have a tremendous ability to forget all the wisdom and potential that lives inside of us, and this is the first type of human being—one who lives in forgetfulness.

Bashar

Then comes the second type of human, called *bashar*, which means an "opening," a "crack," or a "breakthrough," through which we see past the distractions and forgetfulness we build for ourselves. From this opening, we realize that everything in our lives, from our thoughts to our emotions, is created for us by our environment. In this breakthrough, we are looking for someone or something to save us from our manufactured lives. These are the moments when we desire light, to be transformed from the inside.

But initially, when you're broken, it goes against your system, against complacency and feeling good about yourself, feeling relevant and significant. What usually happens is that at first you have lots of friends and a companion that loves you and whom you love. But when you realize that you don't know anything about anything, that you want more than just entertainment and distractions, your companions will find you useless. And though they may want to reach you, you're not reachable even to yourself, let alone them. And then they will leave you, and you'll have no idea why you're alone. And then the internal conflict will begin, and you will have a lot of self-hatred and self-disgust, and you'll have all these depressing moods about yourself, and people will say all sorts of things to you. You'll find yourself condemned by the judgments of other people, and you will want to conform because we are not the sort of organisms that do well by ourselves. We like to be around other people, and we like companions. We are social animals, but you can't conform to this stuff. You can only conform to the inner calling. Because for the past million years, men have been in the business of domination and aggression, making it difficult for a man to rewire his psyche to be more feminine, receptive, and passive. Unless a man can become like a woman, there is little inner transformation.

Initially, when we are broken, this brokenness comes from the outside. But then, strangely enough, we begin to like brokenness, and then somehow your organism can adapt to the brokenness, and out of that brokenness there are moments of inspiration and nourishment. Rumi likens brokenness to darkness and a flashlight to God, or wisdom, and a flashlight only has utility and benefits in darkness.[9]

When something within us breaks open, we weep, but we have no idea what we've lost, and we have no idea what we're looking for. We weep. It's like we've lost something, but we don't know what. What is it that people pursue when they are existentially broken like this? We don't know. It seems that we have to be plunged into this darkness and stay in it, and we have no idea what's going to happen. All we know is that we can't look at our husband, wife, kids, or profession as a support system or a home. Nothing works.

If we look carefully, we see that pursuing the spirit of any religious traditions is enormously difficult, regardless of the name. It doesn't matter the type of person you want to love or be in a relationship with. The relationship becomes almost impossible if you desire to do justice to the spirit of love. Love demands only one thing, which is self-sacrifice. As long as our love remains superficial, we can love almost anyone after spending a little bit of time with them. To be true to the spirit of any tradition is almost impossible. How do you give your free will to a person that you don't even know? How do we submit ourselves to another?

Adam

The last type of human being is Adam. In the Quran, when God creates man, he turns to all the angels in paradise and says, "I want all of you to

9. Nicholson, *Mathnawi of Jalaluddin Rumi*.

bow to this new creation called Adam."[10] They ask why, and God says, "I wanted to put myself into something out there. I went into the animals, but they couldn't contain me. I hid myself in the mountains, but they couldn't contain me. I hid myself in the oceans, but they couldn't contain me. I hid myself in this new creation called the human being," and God says in the Quran that even he was amazed. How could this entire universe not contain God, but a single human being can have God within him? There is a poem by the fourteenth-century Persian poet Hafez that says, "How is it possible that this entire universe cannot contain God, but this two-legged animal called the human being, who falls victim to all sorts of problems in life, can be such a profound container to hold God within? It makes no sense."[11]

All these angels came and bowed to God, except one, whose name happens to be *shaitan*, or Satan. God tells Satan, "You should bow to this thing called the human being." And Satan says, "No. I am made of fire and light, and man is made of dust. How could I, an angel of God, worship or bow to something lower than me?"

Like most stories in these traditions, this story is symbolic, and it is worth looking at a contemporary story with the same message to make it more precise. This story comes from *Embraced by the Light*, published in 1992 by Betty Eadie, who was scheduled for a simple surgery.[12] Though the surgery was supposed to take no more than an hour or so, soon after it began, she was pronounced dead. But she says she went and floated up near the ceiling when this happened.

Looking down, she asks herself, "Who is this person lying on their deathbed?" And then she looks closely and says, "Ah, it's my body." Then she goes away somewhere—she calls it paradise—and in this place she sees twelve men who have robes, long beards, and turbans. They look at her and say, "This is not your time. You've come a little too early. But now that you[re here, we want to ask you some questions. We're going to pull away from this curtain, and you're going to look down. And when you look down, you have to tell us what you see." And when the curtains are pulled, she looks down and sees a homeless man who is completely drunk. And then, when the curtains are pulled back again, she looks at these twelve sages and says, "A no-good, homeless drunkard." And then the twelve men, she says in the book, begin to smile happily because of her foolishness. And

10. Arberry, *Koran Interpreted*.
11. Hafiz, *Faces of Love*.
12. Eadie, *Embraced by the Light*.

they say, "We're going to pull open the curtain again, and then tell us what you see." She sees the same man, but now she sees him without a body. She sees this homeless drunkard, but this light, this sun, emanates through him. And she says, "It's like I saw God inside this man." The curtains are closed, and she tells these twelve men what she saw.

This story from the Quran argues that whenever we judge people, when we say that someone is stupid or no good, we sit in the position of Satan, in that all we see is the physical human being and the literal action. But we don't see the light that lives inside every human being. People indeed forget, but we forget because remembering is painful. Imagine if you were to remember the boyfriend who messed up your life because he was foolish and immature. If you were always to remember this episode, you would never recover and would always remain single. We have good reasons to forget things, but we have moments of clarity despite our best efforts to forget. Regardless of how lowly a place someone may occupy in society, every human being will always have these moments. And the Quran suggests that, instead of acting like Satan, you should always behave like the angels by seeing what the eyes don't see about the human being.

After this, the story of Adam in the Quran is very similar to the story of Adam from the Old Testament. God forbids Adam from doing certain things, he and Eve do these things nevertheless, and then they fall. Adam's origin is a divine place, or as Plato would say, the world of Ideas, a world where only angels and light exist, where there is no good or bad, and people do what is right. When Adam falls, he remembers the place from which he came, remembers that physical life is not his home, and wants to go back home. His body is a prison. Drinking, money, and relationships will always be a prison for us, and the only way Adam returns home, the Quran argues, is that he cries and cries and cries. He doesn't cry because he is drinking or smoking too much. He doesn't cry because he doesn't have money or because his wife and children pass. He cries because his soul wants to go back home, and its home isn't this place down here. Through weeping and lamenting, Adam is able to submit and ultimately return to paradise. In Islam, we surrender because we are so poor down here in this world and have no way to combat this imprisonment except through submission.

Islam

The Five Pillars of Islam

Pillar 1: There is no god but God, and Mohammed is the Messenger of God.

In the Islamic tradition, there are five steps that people need to experience to find unity. They are called the Five Pillars. The Five Pillars of Islam are like the pillars of a deck or house, where the pillars support a flat foundation upon which you can build your life and pursue your desires. It is like pouring concrete inside people to give them stability. Without that foundation, there is no trust or stability. To anchor our life to anything, make sure there is a good foundation. Otherwise, whatever you build will only be temporary. If you want your life to have good support, pillars are necessary.

The first Pillar is called *shahadat*, which means to become a "witness." In witnessing, you become a "martyr" because something inside you experiences the truth or reality; there is no doubt. Whenever we witness clarity, the consequence is that we also choose to become a martyr. At least for that moment. If you go to therapy, what you want is the part of you that is vengeful and poisonous to go away, and the only way it can go away is for the therapist to give you clarity about your history so that you can be more objective about your life and experiences. Suddenly, you stand on the outside and witness the victimized part of you with immature ways of thinking and reacting.

Shahadat means that we are a witness to *La illaha il Allah*, which is Arabic for "There is no god but God." *La* means "no," and *illah* means "idol," or the images of ourselves that we worship daily, which ultimately create suffering and pain. The only object worthy of worship is *Allah* or God. The Shahadat is no different from the Gospel of John, where Jesus says, "The only way to get to God is through me."[13] Jesus's message is, "Don't pay attention to my body, because that which lives inside me also lives inside you." And he will teach you how to think and feel and act. This is the same principle: you have to go through Mohammed to know Allah. Someone who is not a witness and not a martyr is called *kafir*, which is related to the word for "to cover" and is similar to the concept of a sinner. Imagine that someone only pays attention to the cover of a book but never opens the cover to read the inside, and then writes a book about the cover and the

---

13. Anderson, *Riddles of the Fourth Gospel*.

wisdom of the cover. Suddenly, there is a following and millions of people who only talk about the cover, but not the book's content.

There is another way of looking at this. Imagine that you have a tablespoon of salt and a cup of water. Then you put that salt in the water and stir it until the water becomes very salty. Once this happens, there is no place you can go where there is no salt in this water. It doesn't matter where you go or what experiences life gives you. They're all caused by God. You can't go outside of God because you live in the belly of God, which is the reason why in Islam, just as in Christianity and Judaism, the good and the bad in our lives must be accepted equally. For those of us that have had bad fortunes in life, where life has given us some problematic situations, know that all of these experiences live in the belly of God, and all we have to do is to put these experiences within the context of Islam.

The second part of the first Pillar concerns the prophethood of Mohammed. Sometimes God is too far from us, and you can't find God on your own. You must connect yourself to someone who has found God or follow the words of someone who is connected to God. The person who embodies God will allow you to taste the sacred that lives inside them.

To put it another way: the sun or the moon—which is more powerful? Very few of us can worship Venus or Ishtar or Sophia, the goddesses of Love. Since Love knows that you will not reach her, she puts someone on your path with whom you will fall in love. We can worship Love by falling in love with another human being, and so instead of worshipping Ishtar, you worship your lover. Mistakenly, of course, you think that it is your love that you are worshipping. But the truth is, you are worshipping Love, the domain of all the goddesses of Love. That's how important messengers are. They are like a flashlight lit in the darkness of our ignorance. The human being is always more potent than the deity, initially. The moon becomes the symbol of the prophet or a messenger.

To put the messenger concept another way, remember that everything we experience down here comes down from God. Every experience is a messenger, in that each experience is given so that it can teach you something. If you want clarity, pay attention to the messenger, which happens to be your own experience. As human beings, we don't know what our flaws are. All we know is that we are needy animals, and these needs are rooted in the desire to come to life and live passionately. Because of this, the following will happen. We will have a relationship with someone, but we don't know what they do for us or how. All we know is that when we see them, something about us is inspired. But they can only continue this for so long before we walk into boredom, at which point in time we will walk to someone else or engage in some other activity that could potentially create the same inspiration. But keep in mind that these are all messengers who do only one thing, to get us to the real thing, which is the inspiration itself. All the things these people will do for us bring the stuff that already lives inside us to the surface to taste what is within us. We see that we are infinitely patient with the people we love, that we can be forgiving and generous. All these qualities live inside us, but for them to come to life, we need messengers or certain experiences. But remember, we want to ultimately go back to the source, God or Love itself. We want to have all of these qualities ooze out of us, by and through ourselves. That is, without being inspired by anyone except the things that live inside us.

Yet there is dangerousness to the first Pillar in that messengers tend to kill something inside you. If you are interested in money, fame, or fortune, should all of a sudden a messenger walk into your life, whatever this person or experience may be, something about you that used to be interested in certain things disappears. Suddenly you and life will become enormously complex. Suddenly you will become conflicted and hopeless. Despair will set in, all because you have seen and felt something authentic. If you are serious about traveling to the Middle East, finding a teacher, or changing your life, remember that the first Pillar is about martyrdom. You have to be ready to have certain parts of you die. For example, married people experience death in the relationship. First, you fall in love, and things are exciting and lively. Then time enters into the relationships and, like water, drips and slowly rots things from the inside. Time will grow wrinkles in the relationship, and then it becomes sick, where the two of you fight all the time, and then after a while something about you dies, and you just become indifferent to the relationship and your companion. You have the element of time forcing you to become a witness to boredom in the relationship. You walk home. You know that it will be a boring night. This indicates something about you has died by the hands of time.

Pillar 2: Fasting

The next Pillar is fasting. In the month of fasting in Islam, Muslims don't eat or drink from the sun rises to when the sunsets. The source of nourishment is the sun itself. In many Islamic countries, such as Saudi Arabia, all the shops are closed during this fasting month. You can't eat in public, and if you do eat in public, people will be very unhappy with you.

We all have addictions, whether internal emotions and thoughts or external behaviors and speech. Physical fasting is one of the best ways to get rid of additions. When you don't eat or drink, something strange happens to your body. Many of us daydream about the future and past and care very much for what is happening in the present. Yet all thoughts, actions, and desires require energy. When you don't eat or drink, your body becomes paralyzed, and all of your desires that live in the past, present, and future will go away because there is no energy to sustain and nourish them. For example, if you hate someone, try not eating for a while. Once you reach the point of starvation, you just want to sleep. You won't even remember who you hate or why you hate them.

Fasting is one of the ways that we can become closer to God and has several different names in Arabic. One is *ramez*, which means "baby camel." Camels usually live in the Middle East, where there are a lot of deserts and sandstorms, and only camels can survive in this environment. There is no water, food, or place to rest, yet they can go without food or drink or rest for many weeks. Every human being on a quest to be religious or spiritual is a novice and will have no opportunity for rest. If you are on a spiritual quest, you are going to be walking, symbolically speaking, into the desert, where there will be no rest. You will be unable to enjoy food, you will be unable to laugh or sleep, and no one will be your companion. You are the only person in the middle of this sandstorm, and no one is there to keep you company. Only people who have trained their interiors to be like camels can survive this harsh spiritual quest.

The spiritual quest is like living in the middle of the desert, since it offers you no nourishment at all. No one enjoys living in the desert because the desert has nothing to give to anyone. It's a place of loneliness. The sun is hot, representing confusion, sadness, hopelessness, and anger. As a novice, you begin your spiritual quest as a baby camel. At first, you throw fits of anger, but as time goes on and as you mature, you learn to survive in the desert with a good amount of dignity. The world does not have anything to offer you, but you become enormously generous. It's like some of us who have parents who have never given us anything, and we have every right to be angry because all they gave us was a desert. Initially, we threw fits of anger, but yet something about us beings to witness certain things, and though certain parts of us may want to scream at our parents, we carry ourselves in their presence with a good amount of respect and dignity and do what we can to help them in difficult situations.

Another name for fasting is *som*, which means "silence." Fasting means abstinence, and there is something about not eating that quiets you from the inside. Silence can be outward, but the inner silence is much more significant. We have five senses: seeing, hearing, touching, tasting, and smelling. And then there is the other one that is even worse, called our memories, which are the stories of our life experiences that haunt us. For example, you broke up with a boyfriend twenty years ago, and you still have him in the background of your mind, and he won't leave you alone, and every time you get close to someone, you become fearful of being broken again by this newcomer.

How do we look at desires and ambitions and not get excited or want to pursue them? How do we train our eyes to fast, abstain, be silent, and not pursue? How do we make sure that our eyes don't look at people's physicality but instead see their souls with the eyes of our own soul? To create a poverty of sight, we fast by doing what the Buddha said: next time you go out with someone very attractive, look at them and remember that someday they will get old and have wrinkles, and soon they'll get sick, and soon you'll be indifferent toward them.

Every person has their own unique set of addictions. Most of us like to complain. Our task is to fast or abstain from complaining, which goes against everything we've done most of our lives. A man named G. I. Gurdjieff, a Russian-Armenian philosopher from the early twentieth century,[14] realized that every person has a chief feature to which they're extremely attached. Gurdjieff constantly pushed the buttons that lived in his students and had people expose themselves, and they would react negatively to the way they had exposed themselves. Gurdjieff would ultimately say, "You need to fast from feeling bad, from complaining." Remember, fasting is about spiritual baptism in that your senses are no longer your source of nourishment. Ultimately, you have to give up all the stories, narratives, and memories that live in your head.

Fasting has many different components to it, and there is fasting for the masses and there is fasting for students. Some people fast physically, while others fast emotionally, intellectually, and spiritually. If you overthink, you have a humungous ego inside you, and fasting silences you a little by making you feel poor about yourself. This means some people need

---

14. Ouspenski, *In Search of the Miraculous*.

to fast intellectually. All the rituals and exercises that we do, which usually inflate our egos, are baptized by fasting.

One of the things found in the Gospel of Judas is that Jesus keeps telling his disciples that their gatherings and having food on Saturday are no good.[15] You can't eat yourself to paradise. He tells them not to go to the synagogue and to forget all the rituals, but the disciples believe this is their spiritual practice. In this particular book, Jesus fails to create the poverty inside them and can't convince them to fast from their own assumptions that these rituals are beneficial.

There was a man in the Persian world named Rumi. When he met his teacher, he was told to stop reading two specific books, which Rumi imagined profound.[16] Shams told him, "You need to fast from reading these books since they're no good for you. The only book that you will read is me, no one else." Fasting is about creating poverty, and it is only in poverty that you will experience the proper pain, and it is only in the proper pain that the proper prayer can be experienced.

Pillar 3: Prayer

The next Pillar is called *salat*, or "prayer," which comes from the word *sal*, which means "union." You can either pray to the God that lives outside of you or pray to the God inside you. If you pray to the God that lives outside of you, it is mostly ritualistic and called "exoteric" religion. But if you pray to the God inside you, there are no set rituals. Almost everything that you do is like a prayer. For those who have loved another person, you do everything for them because of love and through love. You cook with love. Even your anger is seasoned by love. By the time you reach the stage where you pray to the kingdom of God that lives inside of you, almost anything and everything that you do is an act of prayer. In the Gospel of John, Jesus looks at his audience and says, "You see me; you see God." Jesus has realized the God within, and God seasons everything that he touches.

Muslims have body language for prayer, which has various subtleties. The first position is called *qiuam*. It has different meanings, such as "Judgment Day," "to revolt," and "to bring together." The Islamic prayer begins by standing. You don't have to be Muslim to experience this revolution because this rebelliousness lives inside us. It forces us to stand up and take

15. Bredar, *Gospel of Judas*.
16. Lewis, *Rumi*.

action. Something about you stands tall and says, "No more." It's very focused, profoundly aware, and mindful. Remember, prayer or worship is not about worshipping money or power or relationships when it comes to this. It's like tuning into something that your senses can't reach. So you have to understand how uneasy this makes you feel, where you're tired of talking to people about nonsense. You have fasted, and you realize that no one and nothing is worth pursuing or focusing on. And now, you place all your focus onto something that transcends your physicality.

Revolution brings about a set of very concentrated emotions inside us. Whether personal or social, any revolution has a very concentrated cause, and there cannot be a revolution if something about us is not magnified and focused. For example, perhaps at a certain point in a relationship, you realize that the relationship is not going to work, yet you don't feel as if the time to revolt has indeed come. What happens is that little by little you stand, because the energy that is necessary for a revolution doesn't suddenly appear. Energy accumulates slowly, most often unknowingly. At a certain point, you say, "I want out. I can no longer do this." The revolution happens when there is no longer a focus on the job, parents, or anything besides the relationship.

For example, some of us go to a mosque or a church or a synagogue, or even just a dark corner in our rooms, and though we've been there plenty of times, on this particular occasion, something about us opens up, and we sob like a child. You may think that this is something about that particular time, but that is not true. Pressure has been building up for a few weeks, months, or years, and this pressure finally found a time to erupt, and it does. It's called *qiuam*. To pray and pray the right way, enough pressure needs to be built up, just like any revolution.

The next is *ruku*, a prayer position of bowing at the waist. For most novices, the way this works is, if you've been paying attention, that most of us live in a world of forgetfulness, also called sleepwalking. Once in a while, a stranger or an experience walks into our lives. We have no idea who they are or what the experience is, but they do something to and for us, but we don't understand what they have done. Something about us awakens. That awakening causes us to stand up. We don't stand up because of power, relationship, or romance. We stand up for what these people and these experiences embody—which is wisdom, something we desperately want. We don't know what we want, and because the demands of wisdom are a little troublesome, we usually go back to sleepwalker mode. Then you go back to the revolt mode and then back to the sleepwalker mode, and back and forth so many times until there is a breakthrough at a certain point. You understand what this experience or what this teacher meant, and this bow or bending is symbolic of the grain of understanding you have received. Before, you could go back, but now that you understand, there is a relationship. Something about you understands, but it doesn't know exactly what it understands. Something about you witnesses something, but witnessing something alone is not enough. You need to understand it. Only when you understand something can you respect and honor it. Bow to it.

All revolutions create their own form of fasting, which happens organically. Many years later, once you understand something well and that understanding comes from the inside, you reach *sejde*, which means "worship." It is this place where your forehead touches the ground, and for the first time you feel what you understand and what has come to you from this person and these experiences. Your body does what your soul desires.

The last and final stage is submission, where the praying person sits on their knees and accepts all things. Once you get to this place, whatever happens to you, you will accept. To put this another way, a poem says, "This person has made us poor. This poverty has made us a slave to this person. He has become our home, but he has also made us homeless. In the end, should he say, 'Come over,' we'll come over. Should he say, 'Don't come over,' we won't come over. We are beggars, and as such, we have no power. Whatever is told to us, we shall obey."[17] Another poem says, "The moment my revolution began, homelessness became my companion. If my teacher, or God, demands me to be more homeless, I shall become more homeless. I am a body, but my heart is in the hand of my teacher. Without them, I am but a corpse. But if that is what my teacher demands, I have no problem. There is no separation between God, myself, or my teacher because they're all the same. They have created so much sorrow inside me. But if the sadness is supposed to get me closer, I will fully accept all the sadness given to me by my teacher or by God in this stage of submission. The poem continues, "If God has fated that I be homeless and sorrowful, may they make me even more sorrowful and more homeless." The point is, it seems that for submission to take place, homelessness and sorrow must become our companions. Without them, there is no submission or acceptance, or wholeness.

17. Nicholson, *Mathnawi of Jalaluddin Rumi*.

Islam

The only way that you can understand anything is to revolt. First, there is discontentment and dissatisfaction, and so you rebel. After many tries, you begin to understand a few things. Understanding allows you to become a witness, and you worship the thing you understand, and no one can tell you otherwise. Something happens when you understand and worship, which is the place of Islam. That is submission. Whatever it is that you've come to, now you're able to worship it, you will allow it to crucify the parts of you that are no longer needed, and you submit easily.

Pillar 4: Pilgrimage

In the Islamic tradition, Abraham was married to Sara, who wanted to get pregnant but couldn't. When three men finally come to Abraham and tell him that he will have a son, he and Sara laugh. Though God tells Abraham that he will have a son, they still have to wait twenty years, which is symbolic. It usually takes about twenty years to have any understanding, and when you finally have this understanding, you can't go back to your old self. Regardless, Sara desperately wants a child, but God is still holding out. She also sees a sadness about Abraham because he wants to be a father but can't. So Sara tells Abraham to have a child with the slave Hagar. He and Hagar have a boy, whose name is Ishmael.

Miraculously, Sara too gets pregnant and has a son named Isaac, which means "laughing." Out of Isaac comes Judaism and Christianity, and out of Ishmael comes Islam. That's why the people who belong to these traditions are called "People of the Book," because all three traditions go back to Abraham. When Abraham is about to sacrifice his son—in the biblical tradition it is Isaac, but in the Islamic tradition it is Ishmael—Ishmael has a dream the night before. The place where he is asleep and has this dream is a symbol that later becomes the "Cube" or *Ka'ba*, or the House of God.

Pilgrimage, or *hajj*, is when Muslims circle around the House of God, and a *haji* is someone God has touched. The ultimate task of all these Pillars is quite simple, and the intention is for all of us to get to this particular house where God lives, and there we can find ourselves. This is where wisdom's components guide our physical, intellectual, emotional, and spiritual lives.

To put it another way, imagine you're minding your own business, and all of a sudden you fall in love. You have no idea what this emotion is, and you have no idea why you're acting so erratic, but this is how things are. You want to fix it, but you can't. Ultimately you begin to understand. When this person is not there, there is no cure, and there is no God. You're homeless. When this person is there, you're circling this thing called love. You can be generous, compassionate, and forgiving. Symbolically, the journey of *hajj* is a journey in which, like Gilgamesh, you start with a simple life and a place of privilege. An episode in life throws you in poverty, and you go on this quest hoping to find someone, and ultimately that person takes you to yourself. Once you're here, you arrive at the last and final stage called charity. You become a lamb of God where you dedicate and sacrifice your entire life towards helping others.

Pillar 5: Charity

There's a story from Rumi about a man who is blind and deaf and comes to hear that his nextdoor neighbor is sick. Tradition demands that if your next-door neighbor is ill, you have to go and see how he is. Pay your respects. But the man says to himself, "I'm blind and I'm deaf. What am I going to do?" So he conjures up this story in his head: "I'm going to knock on his door, and he's going to say, 'Yes?' And I'm going to say, 'I'm your neighbor.' I'm going to ask, 'How are you doing?' and he's going to say, 'I'm getting better,' and I'm going to say, 'Thank God.'" Next I will ask, "What are you eating?' And he'll probably say, 'Soup,' and I'll say, 'Good. Drink a lot.'" So the guy goes in with all these assumptions, knocks on the door, and his neighbor opens up, and the man asks, "How are you doing?" The neighbor, the sick guy, says, "I'm dying." The guy replies, "Thanks be to God!," then he asks, "What are you eating?" The neighbor replies, "Poison." And the guy says, "Good. Drink a lot of it!" Then the deaf guy goes home and, incredibly proud of himself, says to himself, "I've done my job." And the sick guy says, "What was that?"

To those who are thirsty, give them drinks. To those that are hungry, could you provide them with food? Charity ultimately means one thing. Study the people around you and give them what they need for physical, intellectual, spiritual, and emotional growth. That is what charity is. Some people are poor, and they need money, and that's what you give them. Some people are poor intellectually, and you have to provide them with different nourishment.

If someone comes to you and says, "I'm not feeling good today," don't say, "Well, there is a philosophy of sadness that says that we should not live in the past or future, and we should live in the moment. Focus on your breath, breathe in and breathe out, and then you will no longer be angry or sad." That's not what you should give to a friend who wants to be heard. Before we give anything to anybody, we should know what it is exactly that they want and need. Don't give them something they don't need or want, because then this exchange will be all about you, not them.

In the Gospel of Mark, when people are hungry, Jesus does not say to them, "Man does not live by bread alone." He says, "Give them some bread. If there is no bread, we can multiply some bread." Some of us make sandwiches, then go to parks and pass the sandwiches out because many people are poor and hungry. You don't hand out Bibles to hungry people; you hand out sandwiches—that is the real Bible for these people.

How Do You Fast from Experiences?

For the longest time in human history, for example, there was no word for "I." Instead, the word "we" was used in many ancient and traditional languages. When we would go to gatherings and someone said "I" a lot, we would look upon that person a little negatively, like they have an inflated ego and they should be more humble.

A man was put in prison and tortured for about fifteen years when Iran's Islamic regime came about. They put hot iron onto his back and lashed him. He said, "The only way I could survive fifteen years of enormous torture was always to fantasize that I am not my body and that 'I' didn't exist."

One of the ways to get rid of negative experiences that are so deeply imprinted upon our consciousness is by making ourselves less significant, less important, and less relevant. How old are we in comparison to this planet? How many people live on this Earth? About eight billion. What are the life experiences of people on this planet? For the most part, quite horrific. It is important to remember our experiences, but to have them guide and control our behavior and lives is another story.

However, this perspective is coming from a place of privilege. When someone has had genuinely traumatic experiences, it's cruel to look at this person and say, "Be a better Muslim or a Christian or a Hindu. Experiences don't mean anything. You are your soul, and your soul is open and free and untarnished by experiences."

People usually have their own time tables, and it's not a bad idea to have tools. It's not a bad idea to accumulate all these ideas and tools so that one day, whether you're twenty-seven or one hundred and twenty-seven, you'll wake up and say, "You know what, I just don't want to do this anymore." You'll go to your psychological garage, look at your shelf, grab one or more of your tools, and all of a sudden you're changing things. No one knows when this will happen, especially in modern cultures and modern people, where we are so self-involved and, despite all the self-help books, no one knows how to get rid of negative experiences. In cultures where people don't see themselves as significant, there is not an idea that life owes them anything. Today everyone expects to be happy, which is ridiculous, especially since life has been a problematic entity for all of us. There is no happiness; there are just bigger or smaller problems and difficulties.

Whatever our negative experiences are, and in whatever ways we are dealing with these experiences, fasting is a good experiment. For a week, if you can, don't eat or drink from the moment the sun comes up to the moment. Make yourself some food, so when the sun sets, you can eat. Summertime is best for people who have peculiar addictions. Just wait until the sun sets, which is at like 9 o'clock, then after 9 you can do whatever.

Something amazing is going to happen. When you starve your physical body, you realize you don't have the energy to haul this body around. You just want to take it to bed and let it rest. And then while you're in bed, you're fantasizing about all sorts of things, and then you realize that thinking and fantasizing demand energy, but you have had no food! Even fantasizing and playing with all these stories is too much work! So eventually you'll collapse, and if you do this the right way, you'll realize when you're fasting there comes the point where you don't want to watch television, you don't want to talk to anyone, and you don't want to see anyone. You're irritated, agitated, frustrated, and want to break your fast, but you can't. So you're just angry! You're angry because you can't do anything! And then when the sun sets, you begin to do everything, but then you say, "What am I doing this for?" You don't have to look at this as a spiritual exercise. If you want to quick smoking or drinking or whatever you do regularly, starve your body, and once your body falls apart, all the desires of the body and mind will also fall apart. And you won't even have enough energy to think about things. And your best friends will come to you and say, "Hey, you want to do something?" and it'll upset you, and you'll realize that you don't want to be around people. It's beautiful! Even if you like to read a lot of books and talk about all the things that you've read, you won't even want to do that.

Fast for a couple of weeks. Then you really won't have the energy to entertain the things we usually entertain, and they'll fade.

But keep in mind that someone who wants to recover from negative experiences, whether it's an alcoholic or an ex-boyfriend, must be very devoted to the idea of change. To be good at anything, we have to take extreme measures, and it's impossible otherwise. When we try to be good at anything, we realize that we can't see our friends very often, can't watch TV very often, and can't have a job unrelated to what we want to do. You have to be very focused. That focus makes you an extremist. It's another way of defining fasting. Fasting makes you an extremist.

Why Should We Fast from Experiences? Why Can't We Turn Them into Tools for Wisdom?

We are not equipped to learn immediately from experiences and turn them into wisdom. For most of us, it takes twenty years to be proficient in playing the piano or violin, and likewise, it is challenging to study experiences very well. Consider the experience of wanting to be in a relationship. Why do people want to be in a relationship? By the time you understand the reasons, process them, accept them, and then apply your understanding, you will be an old person no longer wanting to be in a relationship. The nice thing about regret is that it makes you a messenger for others. We can't transform experiences into wisdom immediately; it takes many years.

How Do You Protect Yourself from Social Forces, and What Is Praying for Yourself?

Let's say that you have always desired to reflect on things or wanted to stay in your room for two or three weeks and be creative. And let's say you've tried it, but you've consistently failed because of various distractions. There is your email, the text, the video game, and everything else. And then you fall in love, but then are broken because the person didn't want to be with you. Or let's just say that your father passes away. And all of a sudden, organically, you're not interested in your email. Organically, you don't want to leave your room. You simply sit in your room and talk to yourself, think about yourself and different things. The only way that you're able to separate from society is for a great tragedy to walk into your life, such as your heart being broken, or your mom passing away, or realizing that you have cancer—it doesn't matter. If you look at all religious traditions, especially religious heroes, something immensely tragic happens in their lives. These are not intellectual things—these people *feel* this stuff.

Pain is your protection against the manipulative forces of society, and it is the only way to distance yourself from all the viciousness and viruses in society. There is no other way. For most of us novices, the statement made by Jesus is quite accurate: "For a novice, you cannot serve two masters." It's impossible. You can't serve your spirit and your physical body simultaneously, and it won't work unless you are a highly evolved human being.

In Chico, there is a monastery with a two-year waiting list to join. When you live there, they wake you up at around 3:30 in the morning, and you go to the main hall, where people are chanting, and then you go into your own room, where you write the Jesus Prayer for about two hours. And then you eat, but no one looks at you, and no one talks to you. Some of these monks have the job of walking around the environment and cleaning, and for them the mechanicalness of scrubbing the floor turns into something sacred. They look at the floor and say, "This is like my mind or heart or consciousness that I am scrubbing." There is a mechanicalness to prayer, but this prayer becomes inspired every once in a while instead of simply being an obligation.

There is a part of prayer that is very mechanical, that has no life in it. This is also seen in Hinduism and their way of using language. First, it is through the lips, where it is just speech. Then there is speech with understanding, and then there is understanding and the emotions refined by understanding. Then there comes the point where you pray because that is who you have become. Aristotle was once asked, "Do you lie?" And he replied, "No." They asked him, "Why don't you lie?" And he said, "Because I'm not a liar."[18] There comes the point where you pray for no other reason than you have become a vehicle for prayer to go through.

No one can teach you how to pray or meditate. We can get some information and discipline, but what you want to happen out of prayer and meditation is spontaneous and creative. Something profoundly inspirational. Rumi was a Muslim, but he never prayed unless he was forced to pray, and that force had to come from within.[19] But luckily for him, he lived in an environment where those emotional states were always available to

---

18. Aristotle, *Nicomachean Ethics*.
19. Lewis, *Rumi*.

him. Rembrandt used to say, "It is a poor way of being an artist to wait until you're inspired to create."[20] He argued that a good artist creates at will. In other words, they just will the art to the surface. But for most of us, we have to wait to be inspired, because we are not trained in the right way.

How Did Religious Culture Become Secular, and Is It Possible for Society to Become Once Again More Religious?

We have always asked whether or not God exists, and we have always asked questions about justice and fairness and what it means to be a human being. But we usually ask these questions in the privacy of our own psyche. In the fourteenth century, the Black Death, or bubonic plague, entered Europe, and about seventy million people died. This was a very religious period in history, where people believed in books like Leviticus or Deuteronomy, which argue that good things happen to good people and bad things happen to bad people. Living in a monastery was a privilege because getting a job was difficult, finding food and shelter was difficult, and no one would give you their daughter in marriage if you had no money and no future. You lived an intensely religious and spiritual life when went to a monastery. The bubonic plague didn't care about social or political movements or individual goals, because when a certain virus hits, it does not discriminate. It is the ultimate democratic leader. Everyone who is near the plague will get it. Within a couple of months, seventy million people died.

Consider for a moment this particular analogy. The fifty-year-old monk who lives in a monastery and prays and worships sixteen hours a day dies a miserable, painful death. A thief who's out there stealing from hardworking people survives and prospers. If you happen to have any common sense and if you're a believer in God, you sit back and think, "This makes no sense. All the monks and nuns are dead, but thieves are prospering. How is that possible? Is this the justice of God?" Suddenly, on a massive level, people begin to ask difficult questions. When difficult questions are asked, doubt enters, skepticism arises, faith cracks, and our identity suffers.[21]

Soon afterward, a man named Galileo Galilei walks into the human arena.[22] Remember what the Bible suggests. God creates many things, but

20. Rivkin and Ryan, *Literary Theory*.
21. Shahzad, "Intertwining of History and Heritage."
22. Brecht and Willett, *Life of Galileo*.

there is something special about us. God doesn't breathe his Spirit into the animals and mountains. Only us. When you realize that you are the center of the universe, it is easy to believe that God cares for you and loves you, but Galileo comes and argues, "You know, that's not true. We are not the center of the universe. We may be in the middle of nowhere." Imagine that you have witnessed seventy million people die, and you're having all these existential and spiritual crises. Then a scientist, in a very rational, logical way, comes to you and says, "Listen. This is my finding. Here are the pictures. Take a look for yourself. You are insignificant. A collection of dust in the middle of nowhere."[23]

Then a German named Martin Luther in the sixteenth century comes forth and says, "Why is it that Rome and the pope claim to have the key to paradise? Why do you need to go to the pope? Why must you be a Catholic, which means 'universal'? Why must you believe in Catholicism to have access to this universal teaching?" This man translates the Bible into German for the first time in Christian history.[24] He argues, "If you have Jesus inside you, if you can hear the voice of conscience, you don't need to go to church. You can just read the Bible. The Vatican, Rome, and the pope aren't important. The pope doesn't get rid of your sins; Jesus does, and Jesus lives inside you." Now you have Protestants, the sect of Christianity that Martin Luther created.

Faith is about God, soul, and love, and when you lose faith, you become all about physical pleasure and power. Faith is about intangibles, but you can touch and taste and smell pleasure and power. Without faith, you no longer believe in the kingdom of God. You believe in your own rationality. Lots of Germans, such as Schleiermacher and Nietzsche, came about in the nineteenth century and said that rationality is much better than faith.[25] For example, someone like Schleiermacher would say, "When you look at compassion, what do you see? Compassion is waiting for the light to turn green, and you see a homeless man, and something about you melts, so you give him ten dollars, and you feel really good about yourself because, for the first time in a long time, you realize that the poor homeless person is an extension of who and what you are. And then down the road, there is another homeless man, and you ignore him. But then you remember what you did ten minutes ago." And Schleiermacher would say, "All of us have

---

23. Husserl, *Crisis of European Sciences*.
24. Luther, *Martin Luther's Basic Theological Writings*.
25. Friedrich, *On Religion*.

tiny moments where we overcome our humanness, the pathetic, bodily, fleshly, meaty humanness that is all about possessiveness, anger, and wrath. Because we are wired to desire permanence, we take concepts like unconditional love and charity and throw them somewhere up in the sky and say that there is an entity up there named 'God.' This God has compassion, and he exercises it twenty-four hours a day. He doesn't suffer from jealousy or possessiveness, and his wrath is filled with justice."

And then there's Charles Darwin.[26] Imagine going to Alaska and seeing a bear with white fur, then going to Yosemite and seeing a bear with black fur. You think, "These are both in the same category of animals. Why is one white and one black?" Darwin argues, "Climate." Bring that white bear to Yosemite. His skin is so thick that he won't survive. Take that brown bear to Alaska. His skin is too thin, and he won't survive there. It seems, then, that organisms function according to their climate. According to modern science, something about DNA and cells tends to know exactly what to do. Intelligence lives inside them. They don't need God.

If that's a little difficult to grasp, take some potatoes to your house, put three of them in a paper bag, and then put the paper bag under your bed. Just let them sit, and after two, three, four, five months you'll see all these flies in your room, and you'll have no idea why! You check the windows, but they're closed. You say, "Where are these coming from?" Then, all of a sudden, you remember that you put these bags of potatoes under the bed. The bag has been torn to pieces, and these potatoes have changed their chemistry and become a home to these flies. Was it an act of God? No. If you leave the potato there, the chemistry changes from the inside. It knows how to adapt. The potato knows about the assaults of space and time, and it doesn't care about being a potato because now it can live differently. It becomes home to flies. And that was how human beings came about. There are currently people who have tails, and we have no idea why we have an appendix. It's of no use, and yet we have it nevertheless. The point is that it seems that throughout history something about our organism knows how to adapt. Just as a spaceship flies higher and higher and gets rid of certain parts of itself, it seems that that's how we have evolved throughout history. If that's the case, it proves that there is no reason for God to exist. Is it also not true that there is something about you that's intelligent? That maybe not now, but ten years from now, you'll understand something has bothered you for the past twenty years? How does this happen? Is it God giving you a

---

26. Darwin, *On the Origin of Species*.

revelation? Probably not. Something about you shifts and psychologically, emotionally, intellectually you're able to put these pieces together and say, "Ah!"

And then something even more devastating happens, which is the rise of urbanism around the eigtheenth century. Forget that England and France have been at war for about a hundred years and that science comes about and says, "We have the answers to all human problems." Because of economic pressures, village life is no longer suitable, and massive cities are created.

Imagine this. When you live in Wyoming, and your parents have a property of about a hundred and twenty acres, with a few cows, a couple of sheep, and roosters, the daily advertisements consist of horses, hay, water, and open space. Should you choose to stay in this tiny village, these advertisements will nourish you for the rest of your life. All of a sudden, you get a letter from a friend: "I live in Oakland. This place is so different. You have to come here and experience it because this is where life is. This is where happiness is. This is where you can find yourself." Remember, in Wyoming, you don't suffer from too many losses. Your parents work you to death, but they love you, and you love them. All your family lives in the same village, and you see them daily. You have your buddies, and you drink, but moderately. The elements of shame and guilt are intense and strong in your community, and you're not going to do anything to destroy your parents' reputation because then no one is going to buy your chickens or your cows. So you behave respectfully. Everybody knows everybody. And then, all of a sudden, your friend says, "Village life is bad. Come here because here there is democracy, individuality, autonomy, and pleasure."

The advertisements tell you that you don't need to wait to die to go to paradise to meet Jesus Christ in the city. Every time you turn on the TV, they promise you joy and happiness. Every time you go on a date and get a new job, you are promised eternal happiness. City life promises you paradise. So if psychologically we used to go upward for thousands of years, now it's all down here. Karl Marx argues that this is what we call an "alienated self," which is a human being who has become a stranger to him- or herself. People didn't need therapy, because once in a while you'd go to the confession booth and say, "God, I did a bunch of stuff. I'm sorry."

Somehow you try to convince your parents. First they say, "No," and punish you for thinking about leaving, but eventually they realize that you're moping and depressed, so they sell a few horses and buy you a ticket to Oakland. When you come to Oakland, whom do you have? Nobody. No parents, no aunts, no uncles, no grandparents, no siblings. You're here by yourself, and when you walk around town, what do you see? Instead of camels, cows, and roosters, there are tall buildings and lights, women and men and fashion. If there were five items for psychological, emotional, and spiritual nourishment on your plot of land in Wyoming, in Oakland you get twenty-five thousand. What are you going to do with this assault? Because of the assault of all this advertisement and because there is no support system, you're going to feel lonely slowly, and when you get lonely, frustrated, anxious, and needy, then you begin to live in conflict: "I am a man from Wyoming, but I am also a man who lives in Oakland." You go back to Wyoming to visit your parents, but you realize that you're taking Oakland back with you, and your parents say, "Why do you say and do all these weird things?" And you want to adjust to please your parents, but you keep slipping, so you go back to Oakland and urbanism.

We are animals that need communities of familiar faces and stories, but you're a stranger in big cities. For the first time, history does something. Remember, when you worked at your farm in Wyoming, your parents loved you. When you need money in Oakland, you work at Starbucks, but your boss doesn't love you. He exploits you. And should you be late a couple of times, he will fire you. You have to adjust to this new way of politics because this is not how life used to be. And now emotions that you never had—the desire for power, vengeance, resentment, jealousy—are all new to you, and you have no idea what to do with yourself. Confusion sets in.

Someone like Karl Marx comes and says, "What has happened to people? Science was supposed to rescue us. It hasn't. We have become strangers not only to other people but also to ourselves." Like the Old Testament suggests, "A divided house can't stand," and you and I are the house, and we are divided. Each desire within us gives us something different, and each house remains in conflict and alienated from the next. Marx argues that there is a desire for perfection and equality inside us.[27] He calls it "species self," a human being who no longer lives a plagiarized or exploited life. A person who has a species self has a job that comes out of his soul, and he sees his own ideal image in his companion. This is a man who looks forward to going home and is profoundly creative. But in city life, we become broken people, people who want to put the brokenness together with hopes, fantasy, and narratives given by city life, and it's never going to happen.

27. Marx, *Communist Manifesto*.

What's going to happen to this miserable animal? He needs someone like Sigmund Freud, and what does Freud, the ultimate psychologist, psychotherapist, and psychoanalyst, say? Freud doesn't even talk about the eighteenth or nineteenth century, but instead says that these things happen to all of us, regardless of space, time, and history.[28] There are three parts to us, Freud argues: id, ego, and superego. The id is the most primitive and infantile part of us. Delay giving in to your kid, and he'll scream. Tell him "No" to ice cream, and he'll scream. Observe a woman who has two kids. One happens to be one. One happens to be two. Both need to be nursed. The firstborn all of a sudden goes into shock and says, "Who is this new creature that's stealing my mother's attention from me?" And the two-year-old will begin to beat up the one-year-old. This is not a kid who has understood politics or capitalism or who's been broken by love. Instead, jealousy and these negative emotions are with us from a very young age.

So how does this kid survive? What do you do with everything you want to do with your emotions when society says, "No"? Superego. Eventually, your parents discipline you, which is like the discipline you receive in class or work, from which you leave frustrated. Now you have an emotional blockage, and if you don't have a release, it will continue to live inside you. There is going to come to a point where you're out on a date, and you've found a nice woman, and the two of you are having a casual conversation, and all of a sudden the discussion gets a little heated, and you get angry. And she's puzzled. "What is going on?" She doesn't know that you've gotten angry not because of anything she said but because of all these repressed emotions inside you. They have been there for years, and you just haven't dealt with them appropriately.

Freud argues that this is what happens when you live in society. You get lynched and suffocated by its forces. You are not only a broken person. You're also a sick person. What do sick people do? They look for remedies. In a secular culture, what are those remedies? The most basic: alcohol, drugs, and relationship. You don't drink because it's fun—you drink because you want freedom from your own emotions! You don't seek a relationship because you want a meaningful marriage and family. It's freedom from boredom and loneliness! You don't smoke because you think marijuana will give you a spiritual experience. You smoke because it removes you from your physical body, and you can forget how miserable an animal you are. No one does things now because they're fun. We're all looking for

---

28. Freud, *Beyond the Pleasure Principle*.

escapes. Before, you used to sit and pray to God, but now you smoke and drink it away. But your issues will come back.

According to Freud, the ego uses the discipline of society to express the infantile emotions of the id. For example, if you don't want to smoke and drink and all that stuff, there's another way you can release your tension and massage your emotions. Play music. Be like Tupac. Talk about justice and talk about how you were born in prison. And society will view you as a hero. If that doesn't work for you, and you find that to be far too primitive, there is another way you can release the tension that lives inside you because of society. Become religious. Read books like the Bible or *Daughter of Fire* to enhance your ego. Become a philosopher.

This is a history of what has happened to us in the past seven hundred years, and there is no going back.[29] You may go to church and pray, but there is a voice in the back of your head whispering, "Does God exist? Am I making all this up?" We know too much. Do you know what happens when you put something under a microscope and look at it closely? We often love people because we don't know them too well. Spend some time with the person you claim to love, and eventually, as you get to know them, you'll see them through a microscope, and you'll begin to see the flaws. You'll realize that they're human, and frequently you won't like what you see. Do you know what happens when you compare and contrast the four biblical gospels? Jesus and the other prophets don't stand a chance. Psychologically, you will put these prophets on the cross and say, "He's a counterfeit."

Poverty in Islam

There are four things that Mohammed enjoyed.[30] The first thing Mohammed enjoyed was anything with a pleasant fragrance or a fragrance that inspired beauty. This is not about smells, but it is symbolic. For example, a doe walks around during mating and carries a scent with her. This fragrance is so pleasant that a male will endure a long journey to find the female. Mohammed says that when you look at people, sometimes they smell good, or rather there is something about them that is very pleasant. And they attract you to themselves, but you don't know what it is. First, you think it's because you want a date, then you think that it's because you want to have a conversation with them. But that's not true. This invisible mystery

29. Mahmood, *Religious Differences in a Secular Age*.
30. Bukhari, *English Translation of Sahih Al-Bukhari*.

comes from this smell, and you want to be in union with this smell. In point number one, Mohammed says, "I will worship anything that smells good."

Second is the very act of prayer. We suffer from arrogance, sloth, and complacency. But one of the nice things about prayer, whether you sit and pray five times a day or whatever the tradition, is that every time you pray, you realize the limitations of your own thinking and understanding, and you bear witness to your own helplessness in the grand scheme of things. And for the first time, you realize your own insignificance, regardless of your position in life. You become like dust.

The third thing is women. So the first is something that smells good, and the second is something that breaks your back and makes you pray. The third are women, but it can't be any woman; it has to be a woman who smells good, a woman who forces you to pray.

The last thing that Mohammed enjoyed was poverty. He would often say, "My poverty is something I'm profoundly proud of." And I suppose, to some extent, you could say that all of these are the same. Whenever you pray, it is an act of poverty. You pursue it whenever you smell something delicious because it creates great poverty inside you. Something extraordinary and inspirational happens whenever you're around certain types of women. When someone close to you dies in many Islamic traditions, you go to the mortuary and wash the corpse. There are these moments, as you are washing the body, where certain verses from holy books come to mind. Take, for example, some lines from the Kena Upanishad, which go something like this.[31] Someone goes to a sage and asks, "What does it mean to be a human being?" And this sage says, "That which makes the eye see, but can't be seen by the eye. That makes the mind think, but can't be thought of by the mind. That makes the ear hear, but can't be heard by the ear. That which makes the tongue speak, but can't be spoken by the tongue." So while washing this corpse, you think, "I wonder where their life has gone?"

Next time you become attracted to a man or a woman, something about them smells good. When something about them smells good, they put you in a state of poverty because you want to pursue them. And then pursuing them becomes an act of worship. But now, here's the trick. If you look at this person, their body, as this corpse, you realize that your desire to be intimate comes from that which makes the eye see but can't be seen by the eye. You don't want to be intimate with anything physical. You want to be intimate with life itself. That is something that women present to men.

---

31. Ghose, *Kena Upanishad*.

Islam

Sometimes you have poverty of health, which is connected to you body; sometimes you have poverty of food, which is about money. Sometimes if your belly is full and you have a roof over your head, but your father or mother hasn't been around, then there is poverty of emotions. Then there is this next stage, where you want recognition from other people, but no one pays you attention for various reasons; then you have poverty caused by society. Then you get into a relationship and realize that things are not working out too well; then there is poverty of relationships. And then you arrive at this other stage in life, as the Italian philosopher Dante did at the age of thirty-nine.[32] He said that he found himself in the middle of the woods, and it was dark, a poetic expression of emotional and spiritual poverty.

You don't give out a Quran when you run into a homeless man. You recognize that he is standing somewhere at 6 in the morning for specific reasons, so you give him ten bucks, not the Quran. Then sometimes you realize that someone says, "I'm hurting on the inside, and I need a pair of ears that is willing to listen to my laments," so you give them your ears to address that poverty. And then you run into someone like Jesus Christ, who says, "The human body demands social status, companionship, a roof over its head, and food," but he doesn't care about any of that stuff. He simply says, "Man does not live by bread alone." He is there to give you spiritual nourishment.

Poverty is difficult for the following reasons. Whenever you pick up the phone to call someone, you suffer some poverty, and when you scream at someone, you're suffering from some poverty. There is a tremendous amount of pain in poverty. Your presence in classrooms indicates some sort of poverty. You need to graduate, so you need the units from specific classes. Poor people are forced to beg, and though your instructors may say many awful things in classes, nobody ever says anything back because of your poverty. Poverty takes power away from you, which is, at times, devastating.

In the Middle East, there is a saying that when you go into someone's house, you enter as a king or a queen, as Middle Easterners are very hospitable people. They give you the best of everything they have and treat you like a king or queen. But when you stay there, you stay there as a slave or a prisoner. You can't ask for things that haven't been offered to you. If you are brought tea, don't ask for coffee. Some boundaries or limitations should

---

32. Alighieri, *Divine Comedy*.

never be crossed when you are a guest. But when you leave, you leave as a poet. You go to your friends and family, and you tell them how you were treated. I hope that you were treated fairly in all three categories.

Bibliography

Aflaki, Shams Al-Din Ahmad. *Rumi and His Friends: Stories of the Lovers of God: Excerpts from the Manaqib Al-'Arifin*. Translated by Camille Helminski and Susan Blaylock. Louisville: Fons Vitae, 2013.
Alighieri, Dante. *The Divine Comedy*. Translated by H. F. Cary. London: Wordsworth, 2009.
Allison, Dale C. *The New Moses: A Matthew Typology*. Minneapolis: Fortress, 1993.
Anderson, Paul N. *The Riddles of the Fourth Gospel: An Introduction*. Philadelphia: Fortress, 2001.
Apollodorus and Robin Hard. *The Library of Greek Mythology*. Oxford: Oxford University Press, 1997.
Arberry, A. J. *The Koran Interpreted*. New York: Simon and Schuster, 1955.
Aristotle. *The Nicomachean Ethics*. Translated by W. D. Ross and L. Brown. Oxford: Oxford University Press, 2009.
Ashton, John. *Understanding the Fourth Gospel*. New York: Oxford University Press, 2009.
Attar, Farid Al-Din. *Muslim Saints and Mystics: Episodes from the Tadhkirat Al-Auliya' ("Memorial of the Saints")*. Translated by A. J. Arberry. Boston: Routledge & Kegan Paul, 1979.
Brecht, Bertolt, and John Willett. *Life of Galileo*. London: Methuen, 1986.
Bredar, John, and James Barrat. *The Gospel of Judas: The Lost Version of Christ's Betrayal*. Washington, DC: National Geographic, 2006.
Brooten, Bernadette. *Women Leaders in the Ancient Synagogue: Inscriptional Evidence and Background Issues*. Providence, RI: Brown University, 1990.
Brown, Raymond. *The Birth of the Messiah: A Commentary on the Infancy Narratives in Matthew and Luke*. 2nd ed. Garden City, NY: Doubleday, 1993.
Brown, Raymond. *The Death of the Messiah: From Gethsemane to the Grave*. 2 vols. London: Doubleday, 1994.
Bukhari, Muḥammad ibn Isma'il, Aftab-ud-Din Ahmad, and Muhammad Ali. *English Translation of Sahih Al-Bukhari*. Lahore: Ahmadiyya Anjuman Isha'at-i-Islam, 1956.
Cadbury, Henry J. *The Making of Luke-Acts*. 2nd ed. London: SPCK, 1968.
Calvin, John. *Institutes of the Christian Religion*. Louisville: Westminster John Knox, 2001.
Camus, Albert. *The Plague*. New York: Vintage, 1991.
Charlesworth, James H., ed. *The Old Testament Pseudepigrapha*. 2 vols. Garden Cit, NY: Doubleday, 1983.
Cohen, Shaye. *From the Maccabees to the Mishnah*. Louisville: Westminster John Knox, 2013.

BIBLIOGRAPHY

Collins, John, and Daniel Harlowe. *Eerdmans Dictionary of Early Judaism*. Grand Rapids: Erdmans, 2010.

Confucius, *The Analects of Confucius: A Philosophical Translation*. Translated by Roger T. Ames and Henry Rosemont Jr. New York: Ballantine, 1999.

Coogan, Michael David. *The Old Testament: A Very Short Introduction*. Oxford: Oxford University Press, 2008.

Darwin, Charles, and Leonard Kebler. *On the Origin of Species by Means of Natural Selection, or, The Preservation of Favoured Races in the Struggle for life*. London: J. Murray, 1859.

Dostoyevsky, Fyodor. *The Brothers Karamazov*. New York: Vintage, 1950.

Eadie, Betty. *Embraced by the Light*. Placerville: Gold Leaf, 1992.

Edwards, Richard A. *Matthew's Story of Jesus*. Philadelphia: Fortress, 1985.

Ehrman, Bart D. *Lost Christianities: The Battles for Scripture and the Faiths We Never Knew*. New York: Oxford University Press, 2003.

———. *Lost Scriptures: Books That Did Not Make It into the New Testament*. New York: Oxford University Press, 2003.

Freud, Sigmund. *Beyond the Pleasure Principle*. New York: Liveright, 1961.

George, Andrew, and Richard Pasco. *The Epic of Gilgamesh*. London: Penguin Classics, 2003.

Ghose, Aurobindo. *Kena Upanishad*. 1970.

Hafiz, Nizam al Din Ubayd Zakani, and Jahan Malik Khatun. *Faces of Love: Hafez and the Poets of Shiraz*. Translated by Dick Davis. New York: Penguin, 2013.

Harrington, Daniel J. *What Are They Saying about Mark?* New York: Paulist, 2005.

Hegel, G. W. F. *The Philosophy of Right*. Translated by T. M. Knox. New York: Oxford, 1980.

Helminski, Kabir, and Ahmad Rezwani. *Love's Ripening: Rumi on the Heart's Journey*. Boston: Shambhala, 2010.

Husserl, Edmund. *The Crisis of European Sciences*. Evanston, IL: Northwestern University Press, 1970.

Huxley, Aldous. *The Doors of Perception*. New York: Harper, 1954.

Jones, Alan. *Early Arabic Poetry*. Oxford: Ithaca, 1992.

Kant, Immanuel. *Observations on the Feeling of the Beautiful and Sublime and Other Writings*. Cambridge: Cambridge University Press, 2011.

Kapur, Shekar. *Elizabeth: The Golden Age*. Universal Studios Home Entertainment, 2007.

Kierkegaard, Soren. *Either/Or*. Translated by Walter Lowrie. Garden City, NY: Doubleday, 1959.

———. *Fear and Trembling*. Harlow, England: Penguin. 2005.

Kingsbury, Jack D. *The Christology of Mark's Gospel*. Philadelphia: Fortress, 1983.

Kubler-Ross, Elisabeth, and David Kessler. *On Grief and Grieving: Finding the Meaning of Grief through the Five Stages of Loss*. New York: Simon & Schuster, 2014.

Kysar, Robert. *John, the Maverick Gospel*. Atlanta: Westminster John Knox, 2007.

Lewis, Franklin. *Rumi: Past and Present, East and West: The Life, Teaching and Poetry of Jalal Al-Din Rumi*. Oxford: Oneworld, 2000.

Lings, Martin. *Muhammad: His Life Based on the Earliest Sources*. New York: Inner Traditions, 1983.

Luther, Martin. *Martin Luther's Basic Theological Writings*. Translated by Timothy Lull. Minneapolis: Fortress Press, 1989.

Maddox, Robert. *The Purpose of Luke-Acts*. Edinburgh: T. & T. Clark, 1982.

BIBLIOGRAPHY

Magness, Jodi. *Stone and Dung, Oil and Spit: Jewish Daily Life in the Time of Jesus.* Grand Rapids: Eerdmans, 2011.

Mahmood, Saba. *Religious Differences in a Secular Age.* Princeton, NJ: Princeton University Press, 2015.

Marx, Karl. *The Communist Manifesto.* Chicago: Pluto, 1996.

McTeigue, James. *V for Vendetta.* Warner Bros., 2005.

Metzger, Bruce M. *The Canon of the New Testament: Its Origin, Development and Significance.* Oxford: Clarendon, 1987.

Mitchell, Stephen. *The Book of Job.* San Francisco: North Point, 1987.

Newell, Mike. *Mona Lisa Smile.* Columbia Pictures, 2003.

Nicholson, Reynold Allen. *The Mathnawi of Jalaluddin Rumi.* Cambridge: E. J. W. Gibb Memorial Trust, 1926.

Nickle, Keith. *The Synoptic Gospels: Conflict and Consensus.* Atlanta: Westminster John Knox, 2001.

Nicol, Mark. *The Mark.* New York: Martino Fine, 2021.

Nietzsche, Friedrich. *On the Genealogy of Morality.* Translated by Maudemarie Clark and Alan J. Swensen. Cambridge: Hackett, 1998.

Nietzsche, Friedrich. *Basic Writings of Nietzsche.* New York: Modern Library, 1968.

Ouspenski, P. D. *In Search of the Miraculous: Fragments of an Unknown Teaching.* San Diego: Harcourt, 2001.

Perkins, Pheme. *Introduction to the Synoptic Gospels.* Grand Rapids: Eerdmans, 2009.

Plato. *The Collected Dialogues of Plato, Including the Letters.* Translated by Huntington Cairns and Edith Hamilton. New York: Pantheon, 1963.

Rivkin, Julie, and Michael Ryan. *Literary Theory: An Anthology.* Malden, MA: Blackwell, 2017.

Rosseau, Jean Jacques. *The Social Contract.* New York: Hafner, 1947.

Schopenhauer, Arthur. *The World as Will and Representation.* New York: Dover, 1969.

Schleiermacher, Friedrich. *On Religion: Speeches to Its Cultured Despisers.* New York: Harper, 1958.

Senior, Donald. *What Are They Saying about Matthew?* New York: Paulist, 1995.

Shah, Idries. *The Sufis.* New York: Anchor, 1964.

Shahzad, Bashir. "The Intertwining of History and Heritage in Islamic Contexts." In *Heritage Studies in the Muslim World: The Making of Islamic Heritages*, edited by Trinidad Rico. Singapore: Palgrave Macmillan, 2017.

Smith, Huston. *The World's Religions.* San Francisco: Harper, 1991.

Talal, Asad. *Formations of the Secular: Christianity, Islam, Modernity.* Stanford, CA: Stanford University Press, 2003.

Tweedie, Irina. *Daughter of Fire.* San Francisco: Golden Sufi Center, 1995.

Urantia Foundation. *The Urantia Book.* Chicago: Urantia Foundation, 1955.

Vanderkam, James. *An Introduction to Early Judaism.* Grand Rapids: Erdmans, 2000.

Wachowski, Larry, and Andy Wachowski. *The Matrix.* Warner Bros., 1999.

Wrede, William. *The Messianic Secret.* Translated by J. C. G. Greig. Cambridge: Clarke, 1971.

www.ingramcontent.com/pod-product-compliance
Lightning Source LLC
Chambersburg PA
CBHW070928160426
43193CB00011B/1604